ANCIENTS AND MODERNS

POLITICS
ANTIQVITY AND ITS LEGACY

KOSTAS VLASSOPOULOS

OXFORD
UNIVERSITY PRESS

OXFORD
UNIVERSITY PRESS

Oxford University Press, Inc., publishes works that further Oxford University's objective of excellence in research, scholarship, and education.

Oxford New York Auckland Cape Town Dar es Salaam Hong Kong Karachi Kuala Lumpur Madrid Melbourne Mexico City Nairobi New Delhi Shanghai Taipei Toronto

With offices in
Argentina Austria Brazil Chile Czech Republic France Greece Guatemala Hungary Italy Japan Poland Portugal Singapore South Korea Switzerland Thailand Turkey Ukraine Vietnam

First published by I.B.Tauris & Co. Ltd. in the United Kingdom

Published by Oxford University Press, Inc.
198 Madison Avenue, New York, New York 10016

www.oup.com

Oxford is a registered trademark of Oxford University Press

Vlassopoulos, Kostas.
Politics : antiquity and its legacy / Kostas Vlassopoulos.
p. cm. – (Ancients and moderns series)
ISBN 978-0-19-538088-0 – ISBN 978-0-19-538089-7 1. Greece–Politics and government–
To 146 B.C. 2. City-states–Greece–History–To 1500. 3. Democracy–Greece–History–
To 1500. I. Title.
JC73.V53 2010
320.938–dc22   2009034706

Typeset in Garamond Pro by Ellipsis Books Limited, Glasgow
Printed and bound in Great Britain by CPI Antony Rowe, Chippenham

ANCIENTS AND MODERNS SERIES

ANCIENTS AND MODERNS

General Editor: Phiroze Vasunia, Reader in Classics, University of Reading

How can antiquity illuminate critical issues in the modern world? How does the ancient world help us address contemporary problems and issues? In what ways do modern insights and theories shed new light on the interpretation of ancient texts, monuments, artefacts and cultures? The central aim of this exciting new series is to show how antiquity is relevant to life today. The series also points towards the ways in which the modern and ancient worlds are mutually connected and interrelated. Lively, engaging, and historically informed, *Ancients and Moderns* examines key ideas and practices in context. It shows how societies and cultures have been shaped by ideas and debates that recur. With a strong appeal to students and teachers in a variety of disciplines, including classics and ancient history, each book is written for non-specialists in a clear and accessible manner.

KOSTAS VLASSOPOULOS is Lecturer in Greek History at the University of Nottingham. He is the author of *Unthinking the Greek Polis: Ancient Greek History Beyond Eurocentrism* (2007) and of several articles on politics and society in the world of classical antiquity.

ACKNOWLEDGEMENTS

I would like to thank Alex Wright and Phiroze Vasunia for their invitation to contribute this volume to the *Ancients and Moderns* series; I hope the result has fulfilled their expectations to some extent. This book was largely written during a research leave granted by the Department of Classics, University of Nottingham, for which I am most grateful. I am much indebted to Arthur Keaveney, Peter Liddel, Eric Nelson, Michael Sonenscher and Karen Whedbee for their kindness in sending me works of theirs which were unavailable to me at the time of writing; John Rich and Myles Lavan offered very useful bibliographic suggestions. I cannot express sufficiently my gratitude to Oswyn Murray and Peter Liddel, who read carefully through the whole manuscript and helped improving it significantly with their comments and criticisms. The last word must go to Aleka Lianeri, who not only read and commented on the final product, but who also served as my constant and invaluable interlocutor and trusted friend during the whole journey of writing this book.

CONTENTS

INTRODUCTION

This is a book about the relationship between ancient and modern political thought and practice. Nobody would deny that such a relationship does exist. But since the eighteenth century there is deep disagreement of how one should conceive it and approach it. Since the rediscovery of ancient texts during the Renaissance, a very common and powerful assumption has been that these texts provided practical and theoretical models that should guide the moderns in how to conduct their own affairs. This assumption came progressively under powerful attack; an example from Germany at the beginning of the nineteenth century is illuminating:

> During counsel in Charlottenburg, Oelssen, section head in the Ministry of Finance, animatedly defended the preparation of a quantity of paper money so that debts could be paid. All argument to the contrary failing, I said with immense audacity (knowing my man): 'But Privy Councillor, do you not remember that Thucydides tells of the evils that followed from the circulation of too much paper money in Athens?' 'This experience', he concurred, 'is certainly of great importance' – and in this way he allowed himself to be persuaded, in order that he might retain the appearance of learning.[1]

The speaker in this passage clearly thought that Thucydides could not be a guide on modern policy; he knew that Thucydides could not provide any advice on a modern problem like the issue of paper money, since there was nothing equivalent in antiquity; the recourse to ancient knowledge was for him only a last and cunning resort to convince a particularly obstinate civil servant who wanted to preserve an image of an educated man. Thus, the passage testifies that at the beginning of the nineteenth century there were people like the speaker who thought that the changes in modern society and politics rendered ancient texts useless and obsolete; but it also shows that for other people, like Oelssen, classical texts were authoritative guides that could be consulted even for details of practical politics. During the French revolution, Hérault des Séchelles, the principal draftsman of the constitution of 1793, wrote to the librarian of the Bibliothèque Nationale:

> Charged to the task of presenting, with four of my colleagues, a draft of a new constitution, I ask you Sir, in their name and in mine, to obtain for us on the spot the laws of Minos, which are to be found in a collection of Greek laws. We have an urgent need of them.[2]

No laws of the mythical Cretan lawgiver had ever survived, but the mentality of politicians trusted with such important tasks is revealing.

A different problem was pointed out by Karl Marx:

> When we think about this conjuring up of the dead of world history, a salient difference reveals itself. Camille Desmoulins, Danton, Robespierre, St. Just, Napoleon, the heroes as well as the parties and the masses of the old French Revolution, performed the task of their time – that of unchaining and establishing modern bourgeois society – in Roman costumes and with Roman phrases . . . But unheroic though bourgeois society is, it nevertheless needed heroism, sacrifice, terror, civil war and national wars to bring it into being. And in the austere classical traditions of the Roman Republic the bourgeois gladiators found the ideals and the art forms, the self-deceptions, that they needed to conceal from themselves the bourgeois-limited content of their struggles and to keep their passion on the high plane of great historic tragedy.[3]

Marx did not doubt the strong influence of ancient politics on the very event that marked the birth of the political world we are still familiar with: the French Revolution. But at the same time he pointed out that the revolutionaries had tried to understand what they were doing and to justify their actions with ideas, categories and models, which belonged to a different world; and this, according to Marx, was a perfect example of false consciousness, which helped them to hide their true motives even from themselves. Despite the influence of ancient ideas, Marx implied, the modern world needed new models and new concepts to understand reality and change it.[4]

Marx's comments provide us with the two main issues we will be dealing with in this book. The first issue is historical: how exactly has ancient political thought and practice influenced the moderns? The second is theoretical: should we accept that, given the enormous changes that separate antiquity from modernity, ancient political thought and practice is only of historical interest? Or are classical texts still valuable in understanding our modern world, thinking about its problems, and acting within it?

Let us start with the first question. There are three different ways in which antiquity has influenced modern political thought and practice: adoption, transformation and contrast. Ancient politics have functioned as a river bed, which modern rivers have sometimes followed, sometimes deepened or changed its course, but also broken through in opposing directions. The case for adoption is easy to discern. Most of the vocabulary of politics we still use is ancient in origin; think of terms like democracy, monarchy, oligarchy, tyranny (Greek origin) and republic, liberty, empire, constitution, citizenship (Roman origin). We shall explore how the Greeks and Romans invented these terms, the various ways in which they conceived and employed them, and how they were adopted by and influenced the modern world. But terms do not simply exist on their own; they are often embedded within political languages and political theories. Many of the political languages and theories that originated in antiquity have exercised a strong political influence until the present. The language of political expediency associated with the Roman slogan 'the safety of the people is the supreme law' (*salus populi suprema lex esto*) exercised a key influence on political thought from the Renaissance to the Enlightenment;[5] Plato's political philosophy provided a battleground for liberals, socialists and their opponents during the twentieth century;[6] while Aristotle's thought has provided inspiration to both communitarians and liberal supporters of justice and the welfare state.[7]

Moreover, antiquity provided the moderns with symbols and models. The breadth of uses of antiquity in modern politics is truly unfathomable. To start with, antiquity provided symbols and imagery that created powerful associations. Many of the most important works of modern political thought have taken the form of extensive commentaries on ancient texts or have adopted an ancient background to expose their views. One of Machiavelli's most famous works takes the form of a commentary on the first ten books of the *Roman History* of Livy; the sixteenth-century works, which introduced the concept of the reason of state, often took the form of commentaries on the works of the Roman historian Tacitus, who first expounded the secret motives of absolute rulers.[8] Two of the most influential political works of the Enlightenment adopted a classical background: Fénelon's reconceptualisation of the French monarchy took the form of a sequel to the Odyssey,[9] while Mably's take on French politics was presented as a fictional dialogue taking place in fourth-century Athens.[10]

In 1787 James Madison and Alexander Hamilton published a famous series of essays, later titled the *Federalist Papers*, in support of the ratification of the then recent American constitution. Although they proudly proclaimed that the new constitution was a huge advance on ancient political thought and would allow America to overcome the seditions and troubles of ancient polities, they still chose an ancient pseudonym under which to publish their essays: that name was Publius, the first consul and founder of the Roman Republic.[11] The founders of the first modern republic put Publius' name to good use. The Phrygian cap, the symbol of the slave who had just been liberated in the ancient world, was adopted by the French revolutionaries as a symbol of their newfound liberty.[12] Although such uses have been less frequent in the last century, they are by no means less powerful.

When Benito Mussolini came to power in Italy, he tried to secure his position with a number of highly controversial laws and political murders, the most famous of which was that of Socialist MP Giacomo Matteotti in 1924. In response, the opposition boycotted Parliament, vowing not to return until the circumstances of the murder were clarified, thus trying to force the king to dismiss Mussolini and to affect political change. This initiative came to be known as the Aventine Secession, taking its name from the secession of the plebeians in Rome to the Aventine hill in 494 BCE, as a protest against the harsh rule of the consul Appius Claudius. Unfortunately, given the limited space of this book, we will give only passing attention to the employment of ancient symbols in modern politics.

We shall, however, devote much more space to the use of ancient models in modern political thought and practice. Athens, Sparta and Rome have functioned as models for the most varied constituencies. Sparta has functioned as a model for sixteenth-century monarchomachs, eighteenth-century revolutionaries, nineteenth-century socialists and twentieth-century fascists.[13] The virtuous heroes of the ancient republics, as presented in the *Lives* of Plutarch, provided blueprints of how citizens of modern republics should think and act.

We should distinguish between two ways in which ancient models were employed, sometimes in combination, sometimes separately. Ancient polities, institutions and politicians could be used as models of emulation for the modern world; but they could also be used as models of criticising the modern world and showing its problems and inadequacies. Machiavelli presented the Roman republic as a model to be emulated by his contemporaries; Rousseau presented Sparta as a model example of what was precisely missing in his own contemporary world. Obviously, a model of criticising modernity could also be used as a model of emulation, in order to make the modern world better. But many modern thinkers thought that an ancient model of criticism could not and should not be emulated in modern circumstances; it merely served to highlight the problems, contradictions and possibilities of modern political systems. Solutions to these problems would have to be modern, not ancient. In fact, one of my main points is that there has been a shift from the nineteenth century onwards, in which antiquity has come to be used more as a critical model, than as a model of emulation. Of course, this hardly diminishes its influence and importance.

Finally, antiquity provided the moderns with historical narratives. These narratives could be used as patterns in order to elucidate the present and future of modern communities. They could be used to predict the development, direction and collapse of modern political systems. The story of the rise and fall of Athens, Sparta and Rome allowed modern thinkers to ponder on the problems of political leadership, the threat of corruption and tyranny, the instability of political systems, the benefits of political institutions or the motor of political change. The history of Rome was particularly influential in this respect, since Rome had passed successively through all political forms: monarchy, aristocracy, democracy, military rule, anarchy and empire; even more, it showed a community in situations of stability and prosperity, but also in deep crisis and civil war.[14] One of the most interesting aspects of the influence of antiquity on modern thinkers is the process by which Roman history ceased to provide a pattern of understanding modern developments.[15]

The second aspect is transformation, and we shall encounter many examples of this process. We shall see how the language of Roman law provided the means of talking about natural rights and how it was transformed into a powerful modern political discourse; and we shall examine how Plato's plans to instigate the rule of the wise and virtuous by denying private property to rulers was gradually transformed into a means of creating an egalitarian society through community of property and ultimately led to the emergence of socialism.

Finally, modern political thought and practice owes many of its distinctive features to a conscious contrast with antiquity. Many modern thinkers have constructed their theories in opposition to ancient political theories: Thomas Hobbes devised his theory of sovereignty to counter the Aristotelian conception of politics.[16] Other theorists and politicians have arrived at their theories, while trying to forestall what they saw as the catastrophic effects of the revival and application of ancient solutions to modern problems:[17] we shall see for example how one variety of modern liberalism was constructed in opposition to the revival of ancient political liberty and virtue during the French Revolution. Finally, many crucial features of modern political systems were devised in order to avoid and bypass the evils that plagued the ancient polities: we shall see how the acceptance of political parties as legitimate players of the political game arose as an attempt to avoid what contemporaries saw as the horrors of faction and civil war that characterised ancient politics. Thus antiquity has influenced modern politics in the most variable and contradictory manner.

To come to our second question, there are many different ways in which ancient political thought and practice can still be relevant in our world. In a few, though not unimportant, cases, this is because there are ancient institutions, practices and ideas which could still be of use in modern political systems;[18] I shall be arguing, for example, that the Athenian procedures of accountability should be given serious consideration in modern politics.[19] But, by and large, this is a limited approach. In many more cases ancient politics remain relevant, because ancient dilemmas and debates are still with us. The relationship between democracy, deliberation and knowledge, the link of liberty and equality, the problems of the exercise of political power, the link between politics and ethics are issues which were first formulated in antiquity, but which still resonate in our own debates and discussions. There is a lot we can learn from their answers, but there is also a lot to be learnt from the very recurrence of the same irresolvable questions. Finally, in some cases it is the actual irrelevancy of ancient politics which makes it worth thinking with. If the past is a foreign country because they do things differently there, ancient political thought and practice can help illuminate what is contingent or mistaken about our own assumptions and show us other possibilities which we have neglected.

Ancients and Moderns

What do we mean when we talk of ancient and modern politics? What exactly is it implied when we describe the history and politics of the Greeks and the Romans between circa 800 BCE–300 CE as ancient? The concept of antiquity has its origins in the Renaissance. It was the recognition of a significant difference between antiquity, the time of the Greeks and the Romans, and the time of the moderns, which made possible the idea of the Renaissance as a conscious movement to revive the culture, the art and the thought of the ancients in modern conditions. But, from the very beginning, the distinction between ancients and moderns and the idea of the Renaissance were in a potential clash. If the moderns were so different from the ancients, how was it ever possible to revive ancient culture or thought in modern times? Even more, why should one attempt to do this at all?

To answer the second question first, we have to realise that the term ancient did not have merely chronological connotations: ancient texts or ancient art were simultaneously considered as classical texts and classical art.[20] This double meaning is well expressed in the familiar term 'classical antiquity'. Ancient texts and ancient thinkers should be seriously considered because they were authoritative: they defined the parameters of a tradition and set the standards of excellence within that tradition. Ancient political thought is classical because it has defined the parameters of what is still called Western political thought.

The fact that ancient texts have also been considered classical texts has had and continues to have important implications. The most important, from our point of view, is that the notion of the classic is strongly linked to the idea of the canon. In order to decide what a classic is, one has to define the canon and decide what should be included and what excluded. During the centuries from the Renaissance till the present that we shall explore in this book the canon has been profoundly modified. Many changes in the reception of ancient political thought are the result of the introduction of new works into the canon: we shall explore for example how the discovery of Tacitus as a political thinker during the sixteenth century changed significantly the conception of politics. At the same time, the driving out of other works from the canon reflects important modifications: the fact that Plutarch or Livy are no longer considered part of the canon and are normally not included in courses on the history of political thought is equally telling.

But it is not merely a matter of including or excluding certain works into a largely stable and coherent canon. The very way the canon is constructed and interpreted has changed remarkably in the course of the centuries from the Renaissance until the present. This naturally creates significant problems for anyone who wants to write the history of the reception of ancient political thought, in particular in the context of the introductory character and limited space of the present volume. One has thus to make key choices from the very beginning. One such choice is the decision to restrict the term ancient to the Greeks and Romans, to the exclusion of the people of the ancient Near East. This exclusion, in particular of the Egyptians and the Hebrews, is regrettable, since they were often considered together with the Greeks and Romans until the eighteenth century; I can only defend it by appealing to the limitations of space and time. Luckily, a volume on the influence of the ancient Hebrews in modern political thought is forthcoming by Eric Nelson, and this will go some way towards filling the gap.[21]

A second crucial choice has been the focus of the canon to be examined on a number of Greek thinkers (mostly Plato, Aristotle, Herodotus, Thucydides and Polybius) and their relationship to Roman and modern Western thinkers. This focus on certain key Greek political thinkers is mainly due to the topics I have chosen to examine in the coming chapters. It would have been perfectly possible to discuss the reception of ancient political thought through different topics (e.g. the properties of the ideal ruler, the link between morality and politics, the obligations of the individual towards family, community and the wider world, the relationship between internal and external politics) and this would have put at the centre of the canon Hellenistic and Roman texts.[22] But I have opted for these topics and the resulting canon, not only because they are significant in themselves, or because they allow the reader to perceive the wide variety in which even the key ancient thinkers construed and debated important political issues as well as the variability of modern reactions and receptions. More than anything else, this is because I want to show that the modern reception of ancient political thought, even when based on Greek questions and concerns, has largely filtered them through Rome. To give an example, the vocabulary of political rule (chapter I), which was essentially a Greek preoccupation, showed already in antiquity significant modifications through its application to Roman politics; and many modern thinkers conceived and modified this vocabulary through focusing on Roman history.

Let us now come to the other question. The distinction between ancients and moderns has been conceived in very different ways.[23] For a long time, many thinkers conceived this distinction as merely chronological. In other words, there was no qualitative difference between ancient and modern politics: ancient politics was simply politics in the past. From the Renaissance to the eighteenth century many thinkers perceived important similarities between their own political systems and those of antiquity. The Rome of the emperors and the senatorial aristocracy could look very similar to the political systems of early modern Europe, whether one stressed the autocracy of the ruler or the role of the senatorial elite. The glory of the Roman Empire, to which many early modern states aspired, made comparison with modern circumstances particularly welcome. This is an important reason for Roman history long playing the dominant role in the reception of ancient political thought.

Added to this, was a predominant conception of history as *magistra vitae*: the purpose of history was to teach by example and this was possible because human nature was largely the same in all places and times. Therefore, the political experience of antiquity, the glorious deeds of civic devotion, the stratagems of acquiring or holding power, or the dangers of political change, were considered particularly relevant for dealing with modern challenges and problems. It is obvious that ancient history and ancient political thought would take different shapes and forms, according to which particular aspect of modern politics they were used to illuminate; in this, they were facilitated to no small extent by the significant differences in the views and assessments of the ancient texts themselves, as we shall see.

But, from the beginnings of the distinction between ancients and moderns, another possibility was also present. Many thinkers chose to stress the qualitative difference between ancients and moderns and to conclude that there existed significant differences between ancient and modern politics. Beginning in the seventeenth century with Hobbes and culminating in the great debates of the eighteenth century, the recognition of the radical difference of ancient politics became widely accepted by the twentieth century. But different thinkers drew very different conclusions from this recognition: while for some this indicated the irrelevance, if not the harmful effects of ancient politics, to others it provided inspiration and reflection for designing an alternative to the pitiful state of modern politics. The change of focus from Rome to Sparta and ultimately Athens in the last two hundred years is to a large extent the result of the victory of this alternative view of ancient politics, which stresses its radical differences with modernity.

As a result of the novel way in which ancient politics has been approached in the last two hundred years, I should warn the reader that the word modern is used in two different senses in this book, one wider and one more restricted. In the wider sense, modern is used in contrast to ancient to describe thinkers, practices and phenomena of the period from roughly the sixteenth century to the present. In the restricted sense, it is used to distinguish between the early modern period, from roughly the sixteenth century to the end of the eighteenth, and the modern period comprising the nineteenth and twentieth centuries.

To conclude: it should be emphasised that the terms ancient and modern politics are problematic. There is not a single thing that can be called ancient politics: ancient polities were very different from each other; ancient political theories could be widely divergent; and antiquity has provided models for the most different modern regimes or theoretical systems. In a way, we can speak of ancient politics as a distinct unity only when we make a contrast with some ideas and practices which are specifically modern; the unity of ancient politics is almost completely retrospective. This is an important qualification, which we will have to always bear in mind.

What is politics?

A last preliminary issue remains to be settled. What exactly do we mean by politics? Politics is a Greek word which means the affairs of the *polis*. The word polis is a fundamental category of the ancient Greek vocabulary.[24] It can be translated in a variety of different ways in modern languages, depending on the shade of emphasis. Thus, polis means a community, and even more a political community: in modern parlance it is usually the word state which expresses the same concept. At the same time, polis means city: since most ancient Greek poleis comprised a city and its territory, modern authors usually translate polis as city-state. In Greek thought, though, it is primarily the concept of a community of citizens that is associated with the term. We might talk of ancient Athens and Sparta, but the Greeks spoke overwhelmingly of the Athenians and the Spartans. Thus, politics means the affairs relating to a political community.

But what are the affairs of the political community? From the very beginnings of Greek literature, the Homeric epics, there are a number of aspects which are closely linked together. One aspect is service to the community by one's means and abilities. A second aspect is participation in counsel and deliberation through effective speech.[25] The third one is politics as ruling. Holding power in the community is seen as a reward for service and wise deliberation; it is a way of honouring these leaders. In fact, even in classical times a standard word for political office was *timai*, honours. All these three aspects were linked together by a concept which remained fundamental in Greek political thought: this is the concept of *aretê*. We shall see that, in later times, this Greek term can be translated as virtue; but in earlier times it means excellence, and this meaning remained fundamental even in later times. The Homeric heroes are exemplars of *aretê*, by being valiant warriors, persuasive speakers and leaders of their communities.

In other texts of the archaic period (700–500 BCE) we find additional aspects. Conflict for power became now an essential aspect of politics. The Greek cities of the archaic period were ravaged by endemic struggles between different factions and between individuals who wished to usurp power and become supreme rulers of their communities. It was the Athenian poet and lawgiver Solon, who was entrusted with power in order to solve the deep social and political crisis that was ravaging Athens in the early sixth century BCE, who first made conflict a subject of methodical political reflection. According to Solon, conflict and the collapse of human communities was not the result of divine anger or of processes over which humans had no control. Instead, it was the result of purposive human action and could thus be controlled through political action.[26]

This archaic understanding of politics remained influential during the course of antiquity.[27] But during the fifth century BCE it was profoundly challenged and scrutinised, as a result of which political theory emerged as a distinct field of thought. It is not difficult to discover an explanation for this phenomenon. The main reason was the emergence and development of democracy in Athens. The institutional structures of Athenian democracy, its political processes and the outcomes of democratic policy constituted a serious alternative to traditional ways of understanding politics. The result was by no means the abandonment of the traditional understanding. On the one hand, the old understanding of politics took new meanings and came to be seen in novel ways; but, on the other, this challenge gave rise to political theory as a consistent enquiry on the problems and dangers of politics.

Politics is a bewildering human activity. Its many sides fascinated and perplexed the ancient Greeks and Romans; their various answers have provided ammunition in the endless debates that have followed them in modern times. On the one hand, one can find in classical texts a profound valorisation of political activity; but at the same time many texts express fear of the dangers of political action and distrust of political activity as a useful means of achieving certain ends. This exploration of the conflict between the valorisation of political activity and the concerns about its problematic nature effectively highlights the Greek creation of political philosophy as a distinct discipline.

The following chapters will deal with these various understandings of politics from antiquity till the present. Chapter one will examine politics as rule, the share and holding of power within the community. The Greeks invented the question of who should rule, along with a vocabulary to describe the various forms of rule. This chapter will study the emergence and after-life of the Greek and Roman vocabulary of rule. Chapter two will enquire about the exercise of power and the difference between ancient and modern liberty. Chapter three will examine politics as an activity; it will thus approach the issues of participation, deliberation and conflict. Finally, chapter four will deal with the ends and aims of politics.

CHAPTER I

WHO SHOULD RULE?

The question of who should rule and the classification of political systems according to who rules are by no means natural to political thought. Many political systems have existed without ever raising the issue. The ancient Romans practised politics and even wrote about them without ever asking the question, until they came to adopt, very sparingly, some terms and questions of Greek political philosophy.[1] To all means and extents the question and the terminology associated with this question were a Greek invention.

As a matter of fact, it also took a long time before the question arose in Greek political thought. Until the fifth century BCE the important questions for Greek political thought were rather different.[2] For the archaic Greeks the main question was whether a political community was well-ordered or not; they thus distinguished between two different conditions, *eunomia* (good order) and *dysnomia* (bad order). The question of who exercised power within the community was irrelevant and there was no available terminology in order to distinguish between different regimes; what mattered was only whether the citizens thought that their community was governed well.[3] The archaic period was also characterised by the emergence of individuals who came to monopolise power in their hands; the Greeks called these individuals *tyrannoi*, from which the modern word tyrant derives. This monopoly of power and office in the hands of a single individual was strongly resisted by the rest of the traditional ruling classes, who believed that power should be shared between political equals. Their slogan was *isonomia*, the equal share of power. *Isonomia* could describe all forms

1

of political regimes in which power was not restricted to the hands of a single individual. These communities could vary widely in their political forms. In some, power was concentrated in the hands of a few elected magistrates or a council; in others, the citizen assembly had wider powers, but only the propertied had the right to participate in the assembly, while the poor citizens were excluded; in others, finally, the poor had the right to participate in the assembly, but not the right to be elected to office. There were no terms available to distinguish between these different regimes; the important thing was that, when contrasted to tyranny, they all appeared to be systems of *isonomia*.[4]

This way of thinking changed rapidly with the emergence of democracy in Athens during the fifth century BCE.[5] The exercise of power continued to be seen as a reward for those who most contributed to the community in words and deeds. But in the course of the fifth century a new contender for the reward of power emerged. We have seen how military service in defence of the community was of paramount importance in justification of claims to power. The new Athenian superpower was not, though, dependent so much on its infantry, traditionally consisting of the rich and the middle class, but based its power on the navy, manned by thousands of sailors who belonged to the lower classes. The claim that the lower classes deserved to rule, because they contributed most to the defence and power of the community, is first presented to us by a fifth-century author that scholars traditionally call the Old Oligarch.

> First I want to say this: there the poor and the people generally are right to have more than the highborn and wealthy for the reason that it is the people who man the ships and impart strength to the city; the steersmen, the boatswains, the sub-boatswains, the look-out offi-cers, and the shipwrights – these are the ones who impart strength to the city far more than the hoplites, the high-born, and the good men. This being the case, it seems right for everyone to have a share in the magistracies, both allotted and elective, for anyone to be able to speak his mind if he wants to.[6]

But it was not just the fact that a novel claim to power could be substantiated. It was also the case that the functioning of the political system had changed in a very fundamental manner.[7] The political and social elite had no power anymore to take decisions on its own. Instead, all important decisions in Athens were taken by the assembly, in which every citizen, no matter how poor, had the right to participate, speak and vote. Furthermore, while rich Athenians had to pay taxes or personally cover the expenses of a number of state functions, poor citizens paid no taxes and received the benefits of these services. To disgruntled members of the old political elite, this looked like a form of government in which power rested in the lower classes and was exercised to promote their class interest. These disgruntled members of the elite soon came with a name for this novel regime: they called it *demokratia*, which meant that power (*kratos*) was in the hands of the people (*demos*). But who exactly were the people? Like in modern languages, the Greek word *demos* can be understood in two ways, one horizontal, the other vertical. In the horizontal way, the people are seen as encompassing the whole citizen body; in the vertical the people are seen as the lower classes and contrasted with the upper classes, the rich, the aristocracy or the rulers. The difference is clearer in the Latin language, which distinguishes between the *populus* (horizontal) and the *plebs* (vertical). Those who initially coined the term *demokratia*, used the term people in the sense of the lower classes; in their eyes it was nothing more than the rule of the poor over the rich.

Thus, the emergence of democracy led to the discovery that political systems could be classified according to which individual or group was holding power. Furthermore, political systems could be divided between those that aimed at the common good, and those perverted versions which merely aimed at the good of the rulers. A regime was classified as a monarchy, when there was a single ruler who governed according to the common good; but it was classified as a tyranny, when the single ruler governed in his own interest. Equally, a regime was called an aristocracy, when rule was in the hands of the best citizens (*aristoi*), who governed with the common good in mind; but when the few (*oligoi*) governed in their own interest, it

3

was called an oligarchy. Interestingly, there was little agreement in terminology when it came to the government of the many. Democracy could be used to describe both the good and the perverted version. The good version could be also called *politeia* (polity), while the bad version could be called *ochlokratia*, mob rule. The ambiguity was the result of the fact that democracy could mean either the rule of the people as a whole or of the lower classes only.[8]

Let us concentrate on the concept of democracy for the time being. The view of democracy as the rule of the lower classes became a staple of Greek political thought and found its most emphatic expression in the work of the fourth-century BCE philosopher Aristotle:

> The argument therefore seems to make it clear that for few or many to have power is an accidental feature of oligarchies in the one case and democracies in the other, due to the fact that the rich are few and the poor are many everywhere, but that the real thing in which democracy and oligarchy differ from each other is poverty and wealth; and it necessarily follows that wherever the rulers owe their power to wealth, whether they be a minority or a majority, this is an oligarchy, and when the poor rule, it is a democracy.[9]

The spectre of class rule by the lower classes haunted many opponents of democracy and remained influential until well into the twentieth century.

There was also an equally critical view of democracy which, however, put things in a different light. In this conception democracy was not the equivalent of class rule, but was identified with lack of rule, with anarchy. Its most memorable depiction was presented by Plato in his *Republic*:

> 'Is it not the excess and greed of [liberty] and the neglect of all other things that revolutionises [democracy] too and prepares the way for the necessity of a tyranny?' 'How?' he said. 'Why, when a democratic city athirst for liberty gets bad cupbearers for its leaders and is intoxicated by drinking too deep of that unmixed wine, and then, if its

so-called governors are not extremely mild and gentle with it and do not dispense the liberty unstintedly, it chastises them and accuses them of being accursed oligarchs . . . Is it not inevitable that in such a state the spirit of liberty should go to all lengths?' 'Of course'. 'And this anarchical temper', said I, 'my friend, must penetrate into private homes and finally enter into the very animals . . . And do you note that the sum total of all these items when footed up is that they render the souls of the citizens so sensitive that they chafe at the slightest suggestion of servitude and will not endure it? For you are aware that they finally pay no heed even to the laws written or unwritten, so that forsooth they may have no master anywhere over them'.[10]

This critical image of democracy as equivalent to anarchy remained equally influential in ancient and modern political thought. But even from the beginnings of Athenian democracy in the fifth century BCE, we come across alternative definitions that aim to defend democracy from its opponents. The earliest of them comes from the historian Herodotus, who described a debate among Persian grandees about what form of regime they should adopt after the death of the legitimate monarch. After criticising the excesses of monarchy and the danger of putting all power in the hands of a single person, Otanes, one of the grandees, offered the following account of his preferred regime:

> But the rule of the multitude has, in the first place, the loveliest name of all, equality, and does, in the second place, none of the things that a monarch does. It determines offices by lot, and holds power accountable, and conducts all deliberating publicly. Therefore I give my opinion that we make an end of monarchy and exalt the multitude, for all things are possible for the majority.[11]

Democracy was a polity in which all citizens were free and equal. Therefore, nobody had a better claim to rule than anybody else. Yet, decisions needed to be taken and these decisions needed to be put into practice. Democracy answered these needs by creating a political system in which all citizens had an equal chance to participate in deliberation and to rule. All important decisions were taken by the popular assembly, in which all adult male citizens had the right to participate and speak. The magistrates were merely executive officials, who had no power to initiate policies or to take important decisions on their own. They were selected by lot annually, among those citizens who wished to hold public office. No citizen could be selected twice for the same office; thus, rotation ensured that no citizen could become excessively powerful by continuous holding of office. The only exceptions were those functions that required special talents, like the military and financial offices. In these cases, the Athenians employed the system of election instead of the lot and permitted re-election to the same position without limit. But even these magistrates had no power to initiate policy and were strictly within the power of the assembly.[12]

It is often said that the difference between ancient and modern democracies lies in the fact that the former were direct, while the latter are based on representation. While there is an important element of truth in this, it is also highly misleading.[13] Many important political decisions and functions were undertaken by representative bodies in Athenian democracy. Let us briefly look at two of them: the Council of the 500 and the popular courts. The Council of the 500 was a representative body: each of the 139 districts of Attica was represented in the council in proportion to its number of citizens. The Council prepared the agenda of the assembly: no issue could be discussed in the assembly if it had not already been discussed and put into the agenda by the Council. But councillors were selected by lot, like the other magistrates, and no citizen could serve as councillor more than twice in his life and even that non-consecutively.

The popular courts had important political functions, as we shall explain in the next chapter. Every year 6,000 jurors were selected by lot from among all citizens who wished to serve as jurors in that particular year. Cases were heard by panels selected daily by lot from this pool of 6,000 jurors. Any decision of the assembly could be challenged in court, and the jury had the power to overturn it if found unconstitutional or inexpedient. The courts were an important means of revisiting the decisions of the assembly, and their decisions were final, making some modern historians believe that they were the true sovereign body of Athenian democracy.[14] Thus, important political functions were undertaken not by the assembly in which every citizen could participate, but by special bodies which represented the Athenian citizens. But, in contrast to modern democracies, all these representative bodies were selected by lot and not by election. Thus, the difference between ancient and modern democracies cannot be sought in representation; it rather lies in the specific role that representation and election play in modern democracies, a point to which we shall return later.

Classical Greece was characterised by an intense struggle between partisans of oligarchy and democracy. To avoid these constant fights, Greek thinkers from the late fifth century onwards came up with a new idea: the mixed constitution. The idea was that one could avoid the excesses of every single form and satisfy both democrats and oligarchs by combining elements from the different constitutions into a single, mixed form. This was a very potent idea in ancient, and later in modern political thought.[15] Plato and Aristotle, the earliest Greek thinkers to deal with the concept, tended to see the mixed constitution as a mixture of monarchical, aristocratic and democratic principles. Thus, the mixed constitution should combine the democratic principle of the lot with the aristocratic principle of election; or it should combine the democratic principle of universal right to vote for all citizens with the aristocratic principle that only certain citizens should have the right to be elected into office.[16]

But a new departure in political thought took place when Greek thinkers tried to accommodate within this scheme some polities that were considered highly successful and could be seen as ideal examples of the mixed constitution: initially Sparta, and later also Rome.[17] Sparta and Rome could not fit easily into the usual classification of Greek political thought.[18] In Sparta power was divided between the two kings, the senate (*Gerousia*), the popular assembly and the ephors. The two kings were mainly in charge of the army; the senate, made up of the two kings plus 28 Spartan citizens over sixty elected for life, discussed all political affairs and brought proposals for decision to the popular assembly. The assembly, in which all citizens with full rights had the right to participate, could not discuss the proposals put in front of it, but only accept them or turn them down. Finally, an important role was played by the five ephors elected annually from all the Spartan citizens, but without the right of re-election. The ephors were seen as a bridle on the power of the kings, and each month they swore an oath of allegiance to the kings, valid for as long as the kings kept their own oath of upholding the law.[19]

Rome had a similarly complex political structure.[20] Power was divided between the two consuls, the senate, the assemblies and the tribunes. The two consuls were the annually-elected heads of the executive: chief among their duties was military leadership. Once the consuls and other high magistrates, like the *quaestors*, the *praetors* and the *aediles*, had finished their term in office, they became members of the Senate; the Senate was the only deliberative body of the Roman state. However, the Senate did not have any power to create new laws (legislative power) or to implement decisions taken (executive power); its role was that of discussing policy and advising the magistrates. Although its decisions were not legally binding, few magistrates ever dared ignore them. Legislation was in the hands of a variety of different assemblies.[21] The centuriate assembly (*comitia centuriata*), which was the one that elected the consuls and other magistrates, was divided into 193 centuries, with each century having a single vote. The citizens were distributed among the centuries in a very unequal way, with the result that the upper classes had a majority of the centuries, while a large proportion of the citizens who belonged to the poorest class formed only a single century. This gave the upper classes a strong control of the election of magistrates. But, from the third century onwards, almost all legislative work was not done by the centuriate assembly but was taken over by the tribal assembly (*comitia tributa*), in which no class had a particular advantage.[22] Roman assemblies could not deliberate on the proposals put in front of them, but, like in Sparta, could only accept them or turn them down. Finally, there were the plebeian tribunes, magistrates elected from among the plebeians to protect their interests against the aristocratic patricians. The tribunes had the right to imprison the consuls if they acted against the interests of the plebeians and had a veto over the activities of the senate.

When Greek and Roman thinkers tried to classify Sparta and Rome as mixed constitutions incorporating monarchical, aristocratic and democratic elements, they effected a crucial transformation of the categories of Greek political thought. Democracy, monarchy and aristocracy were originally categories that described polities as a whole; when they became mere elements of a mixed constitution, the road was open for a radical re-interpretation of these concepts. This was particularly the case with Polybius, a Greek statesman who wrote an important historical work to explain to his fellow Greeks the reasons behind Rome's meteoric rise to world power.[23] According to Polybius, the success of Sparta and Rome was due to their mixed constitution.[24] The Spartan kings and the Roman consuls comprised the monarchical element. Monarchy, in his discussion of Sparta and Rome, did not refer any more to the rule of a single individual; effectively, it had become synonymous with executive power. The example of the Roman consuls, which were considered as the monarchic element of the constitution, speaks volumes in this respect. The discussion of executive power, as such, was a novelty in Greek political thought. Previous discussions, like those of Plato and Aristotle, had focused on participation and the legislative and judicial powers. Now monarchy could be used to think about the implications and problems of the executive power even within non-monarchical regimes.

In the same way, the Gerousia and the Senate represented the aristocratic element; thus, aristocracy or oligarchy was no longer understood as a regime in which suffrage was restricted to only a segment of the citizen body; it was now identified with a specific institution. Both the Spartan Gerousia and the Roman Senate were elected bodies, whether directly or indirectly, and, theoretically, they comprised just the wisest and ablest citizens; but one could easily make the move, as we shall see, of extending this new image in order to view the senate as an organ comprising and expressing the noble and the rich.

But the most important redefinition concerned democracy. One answer to what was the democratic element in Sparta and Rome was on traditional lines: it was the popular assemblies which, at the end of the day, decided on all legislative issues. This answer would thus identify the democratic element with direct popular participation in decision making. It is a distinctive characteristic of both Sparta and Rome that, in contrast to most ancient aristocracies/oligarchies, all citizens had the right to participate in the legislative assembly. This would be of crucial importance for the future.

However, some ancient authors, when discussing Sparta, thought that the democratic element lay rather in social practices.[25] It was the equality of life of the Spartan citizens that was the democratic element of their constitution. It was not the mere legal equality that existed in a democracy like Athens. In Sparta there was a public system of education and all citizens had to undergo the same training and live under the same conditions. There were strict limits on the use of wealth, while citizens dined and spent most of their time together in common messes.

But there was a third answer which would also prove of immense importance for the future. The democratic element could be seen as those magistrates or institutions which protected the interests of the people, the lower classes: the ephors and the tribunes.[26] The ephors and the tribunes were elected without any limit of age or wealth and thus these offices were not restricted to an aristocratic elite; in fact, in the case of the tribunes the patricians were ineligible and only plebeians could be elected to the office. Both of them were seen as protecting the popular interest against the kings and the consuls, and in the case of the tribunes against the patricians and the senate as well.

Thus, the attempt to locate the democratic element within the mixed constitutions of Sparta and Rome provided two more ancient conceptions of democracy: that of democracy as equality of social conditions and that of democracy as the protection of the popular interests. This redefinition of the key concepts of Greek political vocabulary was destined to have a long afterlife. Plato's and Aristotle's version of the mixed constitution aimed to unite democratic, aristocratic and monarchical principles in a novel and unitary whole. In particular, they focused on how to redefine the citizen body in such a way that it would avoid the extremes of either democracy or oligarchy. The novelty of Polybius's conception was that the issue of political participation played little role in it; instead the focus was on specific institutions representing the different elements.[27]

There is one more essential thing to notice about the Greek classification of constitutions and their vocabulary of political rule. Because we still use that vocabulary nowadays, we tend to consider it as natural and often do not appreciate its peculiarities. One of the most intriguing of these is that it was not merely a typological description. The Greeks did not stop at merely classifying different political forms; from the very first appearance of the different constitutions in the Persian Constitutional Debate presented in Herodotus, they were presented as dynamic and mutable. They possessed their own inherent contradictions and had their own motors of change; their contradictions and principles meant that each constitution was prone to collapse and change into one of the others. According to the Persian king Dareius, who is presented as a supporter of monarchy, both oligarchy and democracy are inherently contradictory and their contradictions ultimately transform them into monarchies. The vying for authority and prestige among the political leaders in an oligarchy leads to conflict and faction, from which inevitably a successful individual emerges, who creates a monarchy. In a democracy, the people need leaders to stop corruption; these demagogues gain prestige and ultimately subvert the constitution into monarchy.[28]

This was a very elementary understanding of the mutability and contradictions of the constitutions. Later thinkers, notably Plato, Aristotle and Polybius, presented very elaborate schemes of how constitutions were subverted, what were their inherent contradictions and the process and order by which one constitution was followed by another.[29] Plato was the first political thinker to present a detailed description of constitutional change, from his ideal state to timocracy, oligarchy, democracy and finally tyranny.[30] Plato was primarily interested in the supreme values that different constitutions espoused and the process by which a form of rule was under-mined and substituted by a different one. Aristotle disputed Plato's claim that there was a set pattern through which one constitution changed into another; instead, he presented a very detailed and complex discussion of the different ways in which constitutions could be transformed and of the variety of reasons for which they were undermined. But it was Polybius who presented what later became the most influential pattern of political change. According to him, the circle of constitutional change started from monarchy, which through the excesses of later kings was turned into a tyranny; once the tyrants were toppled, the regime would change into an aristocracy of the best citizens, which in its turn, when its rulers became corrupt and degenerate, would turn into an oligarchy governed by the rich; the overthrow of the oligarchy would be followed by democracy, which, due to the turbulence of the masses and the anarchy brought by the dema-gogues, would finally swing in full circle back to monarchy.[31]

Surprisingly, it was not Athens or Sparta but Rome that provided the ideal testing ground for the dynamic and temporal character of the Greek vocabulary. In contrast to the Greek cities, Rome was the only ancient community which could be seen as having passed through the whole circle of constitutional change. A plausible account could be written to show how Rome had started as a monarchy under Romulus, had degenerated into tyranny under Tarquinius Superbus, the last king, and was transformed into an aristocracy with the abolition of monarchy and the creation of the consuls; the creation of the tribunes, the abolition of patrician privileges and the transfer of legislative power into the *comitia tributa* could be portrayed either as the achievement of the mixed constitution, or as the emergence of democracy; this was followed by the anarchy of the first century and Rome swung the full circle with the monarchy of Caesar and Augustus.[32] This pattern of change would create endless discussions among later thinkers, who gave different assessments of the process, endeavoured to discern the motor of political change and reached divergent conclusions.

As I said above, the distinction between different forms of political rule was a Greek pastime that never occupied the Romans too much. The

Romans spent little time trying to differentiate between the different elements of their constitution or thinking more abstractly of who should rule.[33] What little discussion of the Roman polity from this perspective is preserved comes mainly from Greek observers of Rome.[34] Nevertheless, the Romans possessed a political vocabulary, which would also play an important role in modern political thought. The most important term of Roman political vocabulary for our inquiry was the *respublica*. *Respublica*, from which of course our modern word republic derives, means the public concerns, the common issues.[35] The early modern English translation of the term as Commonwealth gives a good impression of its semantic value. *Respublica* could be used to describe all political forms which pursued the common good; it could thus encompass all three good constitutions of the Greek vocabulary:

> *Respublica* is the property of the people [*res populi*]. . . When the supreme authority is vested in one man, we call him a king, and the government of that *respublica* is a monarchy. When it is vested in a select group, that *respublica* is said to be ruled by the power of an aristocracy [*optimatium*]. The *respublica* in which everything depends on the people is called a democracy [*civitas popularis*].[36]

While this was the meaning of *respublica* for the vast majority of Roman authors, in a few cases it could be used in a more restricted sense. When power in Rome was concentrated in the hands of the emperors, some Romans thought that this was the end of the *respublica*, which was now substituted by personal rule in the interest of the ruler and not for the common good. The Roman historian Tacitus, for example, often implicitly argued that the republic was extinct after the creation of the Principate by Augustus, and he even stated that no-one born after the battle of Actium had ever seen the republic.[37]

This ambivalence of the term *respublica* would be of great importance for the future. It should be here noted that a similar semantic shift had taken place in the case of democracy as well. During the Hellenistic period, the word democracy ceased to connote one of the six simple constitutions and became the generic term for every polity that was not a monarchy, or was independent from a king: thus, it could now cover both democracies and aristocracies/oligarchies.[38] This new meaning did not extinguish completely older meanings of the term, which retained some of their hold in more theoretical accounts, while being rather redundant in common parlance. But the parallel shifts of both republic and democracy to denote all polities which were not monarchies would prove important.

To summarise, the Greeks invented a vocabulary to classify political systems according to who was the ruler; to this, the Romans added the concept of the *respublica*. These different forms of rule were inherently unstable and normally ended up in degeneration; many ancient thinkers came to argue that only a mixed constitution, variously conceived, could incorporate the positive aspects of the simple forms of rule, while also solving their inherent contradictions. The vocabulary of rule was significantly modified when it was used to identify monarchical, aristocratic and democratic elements within a mixed constitution. Finally, we should note the plurality of conceptualisations of democracy in ancient political thought: direct popular rule, rule of the poor, anarchy, equality of social conditions, representation of popular interests or a non-monarchical constitution.

The reception and transformation of the ancient vocabulary

The world that followed the collapse of the Roman Empire, the barbarian invasions and the loss of classical culture, was very different from classical antiquity. The world of the Middle Ages, fragmented in castles, principalities and kingdoms and dominated by feudal relations and obligations, offered little scope for classical politics. But, from the later Middle Ages, the political landscape changed significantly.[39] The fragmented world of the Middle Ages was gradually replaced by two different entities: the largest part of Europe was now dominated by territorial kingdoms, like France, England and Portugal; while in some areas, particularly the Italian peninsula, there emerged powerful city-states, like Venice and Florence. The Italian city-states had of course many similarities with ancient polities: they were governed by annually elected magistrates, councils and citizen assemblies.[40] It is thus easy to understand why the vocabulary of forms of rule, which was developed in antiquity, could become valuable for their political thought and practice.

It is more difficult to see why that should have happened with the kingdoms. But early modern kingdoms had a composite form. They were monarchies in which kings had extensive military, executive and legislative power; but royal authority was often circumscribed in important ways. In particular, most of these kingdoms had periodic assemblies, like the English Parliament, the French Estates General and the German Diets, in which the nobles and the commoners were represented in various ways. These assemblies were crucial for providing monarchs with counsel about important decisions, as well as for authorising taxes and fiscal impositions that were necessary for funding military and civil functions. During the course of the early modern period, monarchs tried to enhance their power by limiting the control of the Estates, or even abolishing them outright, while the Estates resisted these attempts and endeavoured to maintain or even enhance their positions. The outcome of these struggles differed enormously from country to country: while the English Parliament managed ultimately to curtail royal power and to acquire full legislative and fiscal authority, the French monarchy managed to abolish completely the Estates General from 1614 to the French Revolution in 1789.

Consequently, the question of who should rule was paramount during this period. The rediscovery of ancient texts during the Renaissance was therefore of enormous value. The classical texts provided early modern Europeans with a language and a vocabulary in which they could make sense of their composite polities, as well as furnishing a normative standard by which constitutions and policies could be judged and upheld or resisted. The process of the rediscovery of ancient texts and their influence on modern thought was quite complex and cannot be analysed here in detail. It was the rediscovery of Aristotle's works and their translation into

Latin during the later Middle Ages which played a fundamental role in the reception of this vocabulary in modern times. Roman authors had translated the Greek vocabulary in Latin terms; but now Greek terms like democracy, monarchy and aristocracy were transliterated in Latin and were subsequently adopted by the European vernaculars.[41] The ancient contribution to modern discussions of political rule comprised three essential elements: a vocabulary of forms of political rule; the concept of the mixed constitution; and the idea of the republic.

We can conveniently commence our exploration with the towering figure of Niccolò Machiavelli. Machiavelli is known to most people nowadays for his notorious *The Prince*.[42] But it was another work of his, *The Discourses on the First Ten Books of Titus Livy*, which exercised an equally strong influence on modern political thought and will be our focus here.[43] This work took the form of a number of discourses on subjects presented in Livy's account of early Roman history. Machiavelli used the narrative of Livy to compare ancient with modern issues and phenomena and to ostensibly provide ancient solutions to modern problems. But he broke completely new ground by adopting in his analysis the political theory of Polybius's sixth book, which was then only recently rediscovered. Machiavelli adopted wholeheartedly Polybius's classification of the good and the degenerated constitutions (monarchy, aristocracy, democracy, tyranny, oligarchy and ochlocracy), along with his scheme of constitutional change. He also embraced Polybius's theory of the mixed constitution and his presentation of Sparta and Rome as the two most successful historical examples of this constitutional form.

Machiavelli's presentation proved highly influential and set the pattern for similar explorations for many centuries to come. Machiavelli made fashionable the comparison between different ancient polities and between ancient and modern polities as a way of understanding the nature of diverse political systems and finding the political system best suited to modern circumstances. Comparisons between Venice and Sparta, England and Carthage, or Rome and France became commonplace in later political thought. The discussion of whether Sparta or Rome provided the best model that modern polities should adopt remained vibrant for many centuries. He also popularised the concept of the mixed constitution as the ideal form of government.[44] By recognising the inadequacies of any simple constitution, it made possible the co-existence of different institutions and powers within the same polity. Thus it provided a way in which one could construct a modus vivendi between the king, the nobles and the commons.[45] At the same time, the concept of the mixed constitution could be used to resist the growing attempts on the part of monarchs to extend their power and diminish the privileges of the nobles and the commons.

Machiavelli's adoption of the mixed constitution had a significant further twist: it was based on the recognition that every polity consisted of an elite of wealth and birth, ambitious individuals and the general populace; each of these elements had a justified claim to power and influence and every successful polity should aim to satisfy, to a varying extent, the different claims. While he believed that democracy, in the sense of direct popular participation in the exercise of power, was not an option and had its own inherent problems, he was nevertheless willing to accord a strong position to the democratic element of the constitution. In this respect, he presented an original re-interpretation of the mixed constitution and of the Roman republic and its history. Machiavelli added a new element to Polybius's conception of the mixed constitution, which he called 'the guardianship of public liberty'.

> Those who have displayed prudence in constituting a republic have looked upon the safeguarding of liberty as one of the most essential things for which they had to provide and, according to the efficiency with which this has been done, liberty has been enjoyed for a longer or a shorter time. And, since in every republic there is an upper and a lower class, it may be asked into whose hands it is best to place the guardianship of liberty. By the Lacedaemonians, and in our day by Venice, it was entrusted to the nobles, but by the Romans it was entrusted to the plebs.[46]

This concept allowed Machiavelli to present Rome as a mixed constitution, but one in which the democratic element was preponderant.[47] But he was equally innovative in what he saw as the democratic element of the constitution:

> When it came to pass that its kings lost their sovereignty . . . those who had expelled them at once appointed two consuls to take the place of the king, so that what they expelled was the title of the king, not the royal power. In the republic, then, at this stage there were the consuls and senate, so that it comprised but two of the aforesaid estates, namely Principality and Aristocracy. It remained to find a place for democracy. This came about when the Roman nobility became so overbearing . . . that the populace rose against them, and they were constrained by the fear that they would lose all, to grant the populace a share in the government; the senate and the consuls retaining, however, sufficient authority for them to be able to maintain their position in the republic. It was in this way that the tribunes of the plebs came to be appointed, and their appointment did much to stabilise the form of government in this republic, for in its government all three estates now had a share.[48]

Machiavelli saw the democratic element in the office of the tribunes as representatives of the popular interest and in the people's ability to prosecute and judge elite politicians.[49] We should not underestimate the importance of the tribunate as the democratic element of the constitution. The existence of an office whose explicit aim was to protect the popular interests was something unheard of in Machiavelli's world. Moreover, in a world where access to office was restricted to the elite of birth and wealth, the office of the tribune had overt democratic credentials: it was closed to patricians and it was theoretically open to all plebeians. While later authors sought the Roman democratic element in different places, the important thing is that Machiavelli's democratic interpretation of Rome established that, for later thinkers, discussion of democracy would take place with

Rome, and not with Athens, in mind. It was only at the end of the eighteenth century, as we shall see, that Athens came to supplant Rome as the main reference point for the discussion of democracy. Thus we face the paradox that although the vocabulary of political rule was a Greek invention and preoccupation, early modern Europeans applied and thought about this vocabulary mainly through the history of the Roman republic.

Machiavelli's interpretation of the Roman republic was controversial even for his contemporaries. But he initiated a debate on the exact character of the Roman republic that was extremely important for early modern political thought.[50] The Roman republic became a contesting ground for different normative theories of political rule and of where political power should lay. Even more, the history of the Roman republic became a testing ground for various theories of the course and nature of political change. The explanation of the rise and fall of the Roman republic was of crucial explanatory value. Should the rise of Rome be attributed to the wise guidance of the senate or to the establishment of plebeian power? Or to a combination of the two? But even more importantly, what were the reasons for the civil wars and the fall of the republic? Was it the growing power of the plebs that unbalanced and undermined the republic? Or was it the inability of the people to resist the growing avariciousness of the elite? These were questions that preoccupied early modern political thinkers for centuries.

Thus, the discussion of democracy in early modern Europe took place under very complex circumstances. Until the nineteenth century, and even after, almost all thinkers were against democracy as the direct popular participation in the exercise of power. Some thought of it as tyranny, anarchy or demagoguery, while others feared it was tantamount to the rule of the poor. The history of Athens in particular, but also of Rome on occasion, served as examples of the dangers and problems associated with direct popular participation.[51] But very many thinkers considered democracy as a necessary element of the mixed constitution, which avoided the pitfalls of the simple forms. Finally, there were some thinkers who, although not necessarily favourable to direct popular participation, were still willing to support a polity without monarchy or aristocracy.

19

It was at this point that the Roman term *respublica* came to play an important role. *Respublica* was adopted in modern European vernaculars as republic, while in English it was often rendered as commonwealth. We have seen that *respublica* described all legitimate forms of government, whether monarchy, aristocracy or democracy. In this meaning it continued to be used for a long time even up to the eighteenth century. Republic could also be used to make a distinction between monarchies, characterised by the tyrannical concentration of power in the hands of one man, and all the other forms of rule. But in a further restriction of its meaning, it could be used to describe a political system in which no individual or class had a monopoly on power: in this respect it also excluded aristocracy and oligarchy.[52] This meaning of the term republic was also translated as free state, popular state etc. It is easy to see that this meaning of the word republic had strong similarities with democracy. But while democracy was often conceived as the direct popular participation in the exercise of power, Athenian style, republic could be used without necessarily such a connotation. In fact, it was often used to describe a system in which all, or most, adult males possessed the right to elect their magistrates or even to be elected themselves.

Roman history played an extremely important role in this respect. The history of the early Roman kings, or of the later emperors, and the Roman anti-monarchic discourses could be used to show the dangers and crimes of monarchy and the necessity of establishing a non-monarchical regime.[53] Thus Roman history was an essential weapon in the agenda of republicans. But Roman history could also be used in different ways to support the more radical understanding of the republic: the struggle of the Roman plebs to abolish patrician privilege and acquire political power provided both a source of inspiration and a pattern of development for those modern thinkers who were in favour of a popular state.

The English Revolution (1640–1660) provided the arena for a large-scale exploration of these issues.[54] The abolition of kingship and the House of Lords and the various theoretical and practical experiments in creating a republican constitution were crucial for the development of modern political thought and practice. The most notable deed of the revolution was the execution of Charles I in 1649 and the subsequent abolition of kingship and the House of Lords and the establishment of the Commonwealth. No-one in the beginning of the revolution imagined or intended the abolition of kingship; and yet, once the decision to execute the king was taken, the revolutionaries were forced to justify their acts and construct a new political regime. The decision to construct a regime without a monarch was unparalleled: and it was the history and political thought of antiquity which provided the supporters of the Commonwealth with the necessary arguments. While the reference to antiquity was rather marginal during the controversy between the Crown and the Parliament, once the winners of the civil war had to move on from opposition to royal power into imagining and designing a new political system, antiquity had a profound influence. This pattern would also be repeated in the course of the French Revolution.

Out of the many works published to defend the Commonwealth, the pamphlet of Marchamont Nedham *The Excellence of a Free State: or the Right Constitution of a Commonwealth* (1656) was one of the most influential.[55] The history of the Roman republic was consistently employed in order to show the dangers of a monarchy and the advantages of a republican constitution. The behaviour of the Roman kings, the decemvirs and the triumvirs showed that when power is retained in the hands of a few for a long period it becomes abused; thus, only constant rotation in office could secure the proper function of a polity. Rome was not a free state until the plebs fully participated in the exercise of power. This radical understanding of the republic as a free state could encompass even Athens:

> But now, in the commonwealth of Athens, the case was far otherwise; where it was the care of Solon, that famous law-giver, to place both the exercise and interest of supremacy in the hands of the people, so that nothing of a public interest could be imposed, but

what passed current by virtue of their consent and authority: he instituted that famous council called the Areopagus, for the managing of state-transactions; but left the power of legislation, or law-making, in a successive course of the people's assemblies; so that avoiding kingly tyranny on the one side, and senatical incroachments on the other, he is celebrated by all posterity, as the man that hath left the only pattern of a free-state fit for all the world to follow.[56]

At the same time with Nedham, a novel take on the ancient vocabulary of forms of rule was initiated by another republican, James Harrington. Harrington's major work, *The Commonwealth of Oceana* (1656), took the form of a fictional account, which aimed to convince Oliver Cromwell, then Lord Protector of the Commonwealth, to abolish his personal rule and act like the famous legislators of antiquity in implementing the political system Harrington proposed.[57] Harrington sought the foundation of a polity in a different avenue from that of earlier thinkers. According to him, power was based on property. Adapting an Aristotelian idea, he argued that all constitutions were based on who held the balance of property. A society in which land belonged largely to the monarch could only be organized as a monarchy; a society in which land belonged mainly to the aristocracy should be an aristocracy, and similarly, where the people held most land, the polity should be organized as a commonwealth or democracy. Any attempt to base a government on different principles than those on which property was based was destined to collapse.[58] Contemporary England could become a commonwealth according to Harrington only because the majority of land had passed to the commons. Thus, political systems could be securely based on society.

This novel approach had important repercussions. On the one hand, it could further develop the idea that democracy, monarchy and aristocracy could be conceived as a certain kind of society. We have seen how in antiquity a certain reading of the Spartan constitution identified the democratic element with the conditions of social equality. The road was now open to reconceptualise democracy in such a manner, and Sparta, as we shall see, would play an important role in this respect. On the other hand, Harrington's novel conception was a major step in the process that led to the abandonment of the temporal dimension of ancient political vocabulary. Once politics was based on society, a certain society at a certain stage of its development could only have a single form of government. The danger that democracy would give rise to anarchy, class struggle, the emergence of demagogues and finally the return to despotism was a common staple of ancient and early modern political thought. Indeed many contemporaries interpreted the course of the English Revolution, with the execution of the king, the emergence of the commonwealth and finally the usurpation of power by Cromwell precisely in such a way. But once politics was associated with a form of society, this temporal dimension and inherent instability could be easily discarded. There were good reasons for which Harrington's novel conception of the political order would take time before it could become widely accepted; if anything the restoration of Charles II in 1660 seemed to belie Harrington's scheme. But it offered the promise that if a new kind of society based on social equality could be established, then democracy was not only the sole option, but also one without the danger of turbulence and collapse.

Harrington's followers, like Walter Moyle and Henry Neville, defended his view that power was based on property.[59] In the case of Rome this generated an interpretation in which Roman democracy during the Republic was based on the widespread ownership of land by the plebs,[60] while the aggrandizement of the property of the nobility from the late second century BCE was the reason of the collapse of the republic. But in the case of Sparta, the principle that power should follow property made problematic the standard vision of Sparta as an aristocracy:

> Aristocracy, or Optimacy, is a Commonwealth, where the better sort, that is, the Eminent and Rich men, have the chief Administration of the Government: I say, the chief, because there are very few ancient Optimacies, but the People had some share, as in Sparta, where they had power to Vote, but not Debate . . . But the truth is, these people

were the natural Spartans. For Lycurgus divided the Country or Territory of Laconia into 39000 Shares; whereof Nine thousand only of these Owners were Inhabitants of Sparta; the rest lived in the Country: so that although Thucidides call it an Aristocracy, and so I follow him, yet it was none of those Aristocracies usually described by the Politicians, where the Lands of the Territory were in a great deal fewer Hands.[61]

On the other hand, the experience of the Cromwellian Protectorate and the final collapse of the Commonwealth led to a novel focus on the mixed constitution that was going to last into the nineteenth century. The experience of parliamentary government during the Commonwealth made many Englishmen realise that the threat of tyranny was not only within the grasp of kings; even the people's representatives could end up as arbitrary rulers if not restrained in some way. There was thus a need for a strong executive, which would be balanced by an aristocratic House of Lords, securely established in their nobility and property, and a popular Commons. Thus, the concept of the mixed constitution was not so much employed in order to curb the power of kings, as in the sixteenth and seventeenth centuries, but in order to limit the power that a unicameral legislative assembly, like the Rump, had wielded.

Montesquieu was the thinker who set the terms on which the issue of who should rule came to be discussed during the eighteenth century.[62] His book *The Spirit of the Laws* (1748) was enormously influential. We can single out two important contributions that he made. The first one concerns his redefinition of the ancient constitutional vocabulary; and the second the problems created by the size and form of modern states. Montesquieu provided a new classification of constitutions in republics, monarchies and despotisms.[63] Republics were further divided in democracies and aristocracies; their characteristic feature was that power was invested in the body of the citizens: the whole citizen body in democracies, a part of it in aristocracies. On the contrary, monarchies were characterised by the existence of intermediary bodies and an entrenched nobility, which put limits to the exercise of power by the monarch. Finally, in despotisms there were no intermediary bodies and no nobility, and therefore there was no limit to the power of the sovereign. Montesquieu's novel conception of republics and monarchies would have profound effects. Instead of the division between different forms of ancient polities, he assimilated all ancient polities under the form of republics; moreover, his understanding of republics was dominated by democratic republics, under which he included Athens, Sparta and Rome. On the other hand, he claimed that monarchy was unknown in the ancient world, since the ancients 'had no notion of a government founded on a body of nobles'.[64]

The second and most important contribution of Montesquieu concerned his identification of democracy and republic with social equality. As he put it, 'A love of the republic, in a democracy, is a love of the democracy; as the latter is that of equality. A love of the democracy is, likewise, that of frugality'.[65] This conception of democracy served to differentiate ancient democracies from modern monarchies, which were based on widespread economic and social inequalities. Sparta, Rome and, to a lesser extent, Athens served as models of democratic republics, where equality in landholdings and frugality in the use of wealth provided the fundaments for their political successes. He thus dissociated Sparta and Rome from the image of the mixed constitution and the comparison with Venice and England and pushed them towards the image of an egalitarian polity.

Montesquieu was ambivalent in his reaction to ancient republics; while he admired them for their accomplishments, at the same time he thought that they were a relic of the past, which could not survive or revive in a modern world dominated by large states, commerce and luxury. Republics had to be small in size, so that it was possible to discern the common good within an egalitarian community.[66] Whenever republics expanded into larger territorial states, they ended up in despotism: a citizen assembly could not govern a large state. Only a monarchy, with its nobility and intermediary bodies could govern a large state without ending up in despotism. The story of the expansion of the Roman Republic and its ultimate collapse and substitution by the emperors provided an illustrative example, as Montesquieu showed in his other great work, the *Considerations on the Causes of the Greatness and Decline of the Romans* (1734).[67]

Although Montesquieu considered the revival of ancient republicanism impossible, his novel conception of ancient republics would soon prove very popular with people who thought otherwise. The eighteenth century was dominated by the struggle against privilege, nobility and its entrenched institutions. For those who wanted to abolish privilege the ancient republics, as presented by Montesquieu, provided an appealing model of how a society could function without kings and nobles.

J. J. Rousseau adopted Montesquieu's conception of ancient republics and put it to novel uses. The ancient republics provided Rousseau with a model of the political system he presented in his *Social Contract* (1762). Rousseau insisted on a fundamental distinction between sovereignty and government. Sovereignty, whose domain was the promulgation of general laws applicable to all citizens, was indivisible and rested in all the citizens. Laws could only be the expression of the general will of the citizens, voiced in assemblies in which all the citizens had the right and the duty to participate and vote. On the contrary, government concerned the application of the general laws to specific cases. In other words, sovereignty concerned the legislative power, while government concerned the executive power. In Rousseau's scheme, the ancient political forms of democracy, monarchy and aristocracy concerned only the government and not the sovereignty. These terms referred solely to the number of persons who exercised executive power; the legislative power of sovereignty could only be exercised by the people as a whole. Rousseau was not a partisan of democracy as a form of government: he famously stated that 'were there a people of gods, their government would be democratic. So perfect a government is not for men'.[68] Thus, he was highly critical of the Athenian democracy, because her assemblies mixed up the distinct roles of sovereignty and government:

> When, for instance, the people of Athens nominated or displaced its rulers, decreed honours to one, and imposed penalties on another,

and, by a multitude of particular decrees, exercised all the functions of government indiscriminately, it had in such cases no longer a general will in the strict sense; it was acting no longer as Sovereign, but as magistrate.[69]

The general will cannot deal with particular issues, as government necessitates, for it would then be corrupted by the particular interests that necessarily exist in all communities. Rousseau's personal preference was for government to be handed over to an elective aristocracy, i.e. magistrates elected by the citizens for their wisdom and capacities.[70] But, at the same time, the position that sovereignty and the legislative power belong to the whole citizen body opened the way for what became one of the main modern understandings of democracy: instead of the former conception of democracy as a form of sharing power, it was now identified with popular sovereignty. Since Rousseau was writing for the city-state of Geneva, which had a relatively small population, he was not concerned how the citizens of a large territorial state would be able to exercise their sovereignty. He was adamant against representation:

The idea of representation is modern; it comes to us from feudal government, from that iniquitous and absurd system which degrades humanity and dishonours the name of man. In ancient republics and even in monarchies, the people never had representatives; the word itself was unknown. It is very singular that in Rome, where the tribunes were so sacrosanct, it was never even imagined that they could usurp the functions of the people, and that in the midst of so great a multitude they never attempted to pass on their own authority a single plebiscitum. We can, however, form an idea of the difficulties sometimes caused by the people being so numerous, from what happened in the time of the Gracchi, when some of the citizens had to cast their votes from the roofs of buildings.[71]

Rousseau turned to Rome to find a model for the exercise of sovereignty by citizen assemblies. A large part of book four of *The Social Contract* is devoted to a detailed examination of the various Roman assemblies. It is noteworthy that Rousseau observes that at some point there were some 400,000 Roman citizens and then comments:

> What difficulties might not be supposed to stand in the way of the frequent assemblage of the vast population of this capital and its neighbourhood. Yet, few weeks passed without the Roman people being in assembly, and even being so several times. It exercised not only the rights of Sovereignty, but also a part of those of government. It dealt with certain matters, and judged certain cases, and this whole people was found in the public meeting-place hardly less often as magistrates than as citizens.[72]

Thus Rousseau saw in Rome, with its large citizen body, a possible model for how popular sovereignty could be exercised in large modern states.

It was during the American Revolution and its immediate aftermath (1776–1788) and the French Revolution that followed directly after (1789–1798) that the issue of who should rule was again put into the agenda with urgency. In both America and France the revolutionaries came to reject monarchy and privilege and to construct political systems that were called republican. For the American and French designers of new political systems the experience of the ancient polities and the ancient political vocabulary in its various forms was of paramount importance.[73]

The first thing to note is that it was during that time that democracy returned to the centre of attention as a realistic prospect. Contemporaries understood democracy in a variety of different ways. The many different understandings of democracy that existed already in antiquity facilitated these various modern understandings. To start with, democracy was still understood as direct popular participation in decision making. Of course, nobody could anymore ignore the warnings raised during the whole of the eighteenth century that this was no more feasible in the large states of modernity. But there were various answers that could be given to this real problem. Everybody agreed that governance through a citizen assembly was impossible in states with millions of citizens. Therefore, everybody recognised the necessity of elected representatives, who would vote for legislation on a day-to-day basis. But the election of representatives did not guarantee that they would accurately reflect the popular will. There were, therefore, two important issues to be dealt with: how to control and oblige the representatives to conform to the popular will and how to enhance the participation of the people in the decision-making process.[74] In both America and France a number of thinkers and activists came to argue that this could be achieved through a process of popular verification, in which the citizens, assembled in local meetings, would verify the laws that were voted by their representatives.[75] No law should be valid until it was finally approved by the local assemblies. This was a solution that combined the use of elected representatives with direct popular participation in a modern extended state. At the same time, there were various experiments, inspired by the Roman example of the tribunes, to create bodies that would ensure that representatives would concur with the popular will. The radical Pennsylvania constitution created a council of Censors, modelled on the ephors and tribunes, whose aim was to prevent the elected representatives from abusing their positions and subverting the popular will.[76]

On the other hand, the old image of democracy as the rule of the poor was still present, but with a vengeance. In the course of the American Revolution and its aftermath, the elite found out with horror that the political system was sliding towards democracy. The large legislative assemblies were no longer the monopoly of the elite; they often comprised plain farmers, mechanics, shopkeepers and merchants. Even more, these assemblies took a number of measures in favour of the lower classes. They adopted laws that cancelled debts or significantly restricted the ability of lenders to claim back their loans; they closed the courts or annulled their decisions in order to stop the eviction of poor borrowers from their properties; they enforced the use of paper notes in order to provide the poor citizens with cheap money.

There were two different answers to the novel threat of democracy. The one was on traditional lines based on the familiar concept of the mixed constitution. John Adams, the revolutionary leader and future second president of the US, spelt out the necessity of a mixed constitution in his *A Defence of the Constitutions of Government of the United States* (1787).[77] A large part of the first volume of this work was devoted to the history of various ancient republics, in order to show the dangers of the simple constitutions. The tumults of Athens and the fall of the Roman republic were presented as examples of the dangers of an unbalanced constitution. Adams was against the establishment of unicameral legislative assemblies. The concentration of all power in the hands of a single assembly would not only lead to tyranny due to the lack of control; it would also mean that such an assembly would be dominated by the rich and powerful who would intimidate the simpler and poorer members with their wealth, ancestry and education. The perennial war between the rich and the poor, between democracy and aristocracy, could only be stabilised by according separate chambers for the different orders of society. Thus, it was necessary to divide the legislative assembly into two different bodies: the lower house would represent the people, while the upper house would represent the aristocracy of birth, wealth and education. These two bodies would be able to balance each other, without one dominating the other.

But for many other American thinkers and politicians this was an inadequate answer. The American people had tasted too much of equality and liberty to be able to accept the idea of separate orders. As one pamphleteer who called himself Demophilus put it, 'Had the Romans been a true Democracy, without a Senate, or body different from the Plebians, they might have avoided those jars and contentions which continually subsisted between those two bodies'.[78] If it was still necessary and possible to avoid the dangers of democracy, the solution should come from a different source. This solution was finally enshrined in the constitution of the United States that was adopted in 1788. The most famous explication of the principles behind the American Constitution is the *Federalist Papers*, a series of newspaper articles written by James Madison, Alexander Hamilton and John Jay in support of the ratification of the constitution by the separate states. These articles were subsequently published as a book, and remain one of the classics of political thought.

The authors of the *Federalist Papers* were totally against democracy on many different counts. They criticised democracy as the rule of the lower classes:

> It may be concluded, that a pure democracy, by which I mean, a society consisting of a small number of citizens, who assemble and administer the government in person, can admit of no cure for the mischiefs of faction. A common passion or interest will, in almost every case, be felt by a majority of the whole; a communication and concert, results from the form of government itself; and there is nothing to check the inducements to sacrifice the weaker party, or an obnoxious individual. Hence it is, that such democracies have ever been spectacles of turbulence and contention; have ever been found incompatible with personal security, or the rights of property; and have, in general, been as short in their lives, as they have been violent in their deaths.[79]

They summarised thus the differences between their proposed system, a republic, and democracy:

> The two great points of difference, between a democracy and a republic, are, first, the delegation of the government, in the latter, to a small number of citizens elected by the rest; secondly, the greater number of citizens, and greater sphere of country, over which the latter may be extended.[80]

The authors of the *Federalist Papers* thus offered a significant redefinition of ancient political vocabulary. Republicanism was now identified with the election of representatives of the people; and contrary to the beliefs of

Montesquieu and most of their contemporaries, a republican form could be extended to a large modern state. They were aware that representation was not unknown in antiquity, but they were adamant that in America it would play a different role:

> It is clear, that the principle of representation was neither unknown to the ancients, nor wholly overlooked in their political constitutions. The true distinction between these and the American governments, lies *in the total exclusion of the people, in their collective capacity, from any share in the latter*, and not in the *total exclusion of the representatives of the people* from the administration of the *former*. The distinction, however, thus qualified, must be admitted to leave a most advantageous superiority in favour of the United States. But to insure to this advantage its full effect, we must be careful not to separate it from the other advantage, of an extensive territory. For it cannot be believed, that any form of representative government could have succeeded within the narrow limits occupied by the democracies of Greece.[81]

What the Federalists meant by this was that representation was not just the pragmatic acceptance of the fact that modern states were too large to allow direct citizen participation.[82] Instead, election and representation on a large scale would play the role that previous thinkers had entrusted to the mixed constitution. They realised that the American people would not be willing to accept that the stability of the polity necessitated that the chamber of the representatives of the people must be balanced by a chamber of senators for life standing for the interests of the upper classes. The creation of a federal House of Representatives was the outcome of this realisation. Shopkeepers, farmers and artisans still had a chance to be elected as representatives in the small electoral districts of the individual States. But the huge electoral districts of the new federal Congress meant that only people who were widely known for their birth, wealth and achievements stood a chance of being elected. The Federalists were aware of the ancient maxim that election was an oligarchic measure of distributing power. The selection by vote of the natural aristocracy of wealth, birth and education would thus secure both popular legitimacy and at the same time the filtering of the popular wishes:

> The effect of the first difference is, on the one hand, to refine and enlarge the public views, by passing them through the medium of a chosen body of citizens, whose wisdom may best discern the true interest of their country, and whose patriotism and love of justice, will be least likely to sacrifice it to temporary or partial considerations.[83]

Thus, representative government was invented as a conscious counter-solution to the threat of democracy, understood as direct popular participation in decision-making and as the rule of the poor.[84] In the course of the nineteenth and twentieth centuries, this form of government has become dominant over the whole world. The most common appellation for this system nowadays is representative democracy: but why did a form of government that was invented as an antidote to democracy eventually come to be considered as a species, if not the quintessence, of democracy?

To understand this we have to turn to the other understandings of democracy that were generated in antiquity or in modern reflections on antiquity.[85] We have seen how democracy was variously identified with a non-monarchical polity, the equality of social conditions or the representation of popular interests. And it is through the French Revolution that these understandings came to prominence. On the Fourth of August 1789, the French Constituent Assembly abolished all feudal privileges, creating a society of civil equality. This was widely seen as the birth of a new era, the emergence of a new kind of society based on equality and unburdened by privilege. The French Revolution did not of course create social equality, but from the perspective of an *ancien régime* society, where the nobility held an enormous amount of wealth and power due to its legal and social privileges, the new society was distinctly egalitarian. Every thinker, no matter whether he deplored or endorsed the radical changes signalled by the French revolution, agreed that the old form of society could not be brought back to life or withstand the test of time, where it still existed; the new form of society was in search of a new form of political system. Montesquieu had described how the *ancien régime* was a monarchy based on an entrenched nobility and social inequality. The *ancien régime* had fallen, but the French revolutionaries found themselves in a titanic struggle with its supporters. In the fight against counter-revolution, the revolutionaries brought back to life a word from the ancient vocabulary to describe their opponents: they were called aristocrats, supporters of the privileged old order. Thus, the victory of the opponents of aristocracy could not be anything but the victory of democracy.

It is at this point that the view of ancient republics as based on equality and love of country, which we saw in Montesquieu, moved out of its restriction to a long-gone past and emerged as a model for arranging the modern egalitarian societies.[86] The idea that democracy was a kind of society based on social equality became widespread, even though there was large disagreement whether ancient and modern equality and liberty coincided or differed radically. The major statement that identified the new society with democracy was Alexis de Tocqueville's *Democracy in America* (1835–1840).[87] Influenced by Montesquieu,[88] Tocqueville argued that the new form of society could ultimately only take the form of democracy. The quest over the merits of different political regimes was for him over.

The fight to give to the lower classes the right to vote and protect their interests is another important reason why the regimes that were the result of the achievement of universal suffrage were thought of as democracies. In contrast to America, where the majority of adult males had the suffrage by the beginning of the Revolution, in Europe the fight to gain the vote would dominate the century that followed the French revolution. This view of democracy, and the struggle to enforce it, was heavily influenced by antiquity. In fact, it had both a Greek and a Roman side. The most impressive evidence for the influence that Roman history still held in the nineteenth century concerns the struggle for the extension of the suffrage in France. It was then that socialist thinkers used the term proletarian to describe the working classes who lacked the vote. The proletarians, so called because, due to their poverty, they could not buy their military equipment and their only contribution to the community were their offspring (*proles*), were the sixth and last class of the Roman census: though they comprised the largest part of the population, they formed only one out of the 193 centuries, and were thus effectively disfranchised.[89] Those excluded from the suffrage came to identify themselves with a social group through a reading of Roman history. Thus, the achievement of universal suffrage for all adult males during the nineteenth and early twentieth centuries came to be seen as the victory of democracy, both in the affirmation of popular sovereignty and in the final achievement of the representation of popular interests.

One good example of how the term democracy now became pre-eminent as a description of a popular state is the republication in 1796 of Walter Moyle's *Essay on the Roman Government* by the English Jacobin John Thelwall. Characteristically, Thelwall added the following two words at the beginning of the title: 'Democracy vindicated'. As he noted in the preface, his purpose was 'the complete vindication of popular government . . . against the oft reiterated, but unfounded, charge of violence and depredation' and to show that 'those cities are always freest from disturbances, in which there are no sprigs and strips of nobility'.[90] During the prohibition of public political association in the 1790's Thelwall toured the country lecturing on Roman history as a cover for spreading democratic ideas.[91]

It was within this context that Rome was finally supplanted by Athens and Athenian democracy became the quintessential reference point of ancient democracies.[92] The process started in Britain, when a number of authors who were strongly opposed to the American and French Revolutions used Greek history in order to warn about the dangers of the return of democracy. This politicisation of Greek history was novel and it caught the mood of the times: William Mitford's *History of Greece* (1784–1806) became one of the most influential historical and political works in the fifty years between 1780 and 1830. The negative lessons of Athenian democracy were seized upon by all who opposed the extension of the franchise in the beginning of the nineteenth century: Athenian history proved that democracy was the equivalent of anarchy, mob rule and the tyranny of the poor over the rich. The supporters of the reform acts and the liberalisation of British politics soon came to turn the tables and use Athens as a model of the political system they espoused. George Grote, a banker and radical MP in the 1820's and 1830's, composed a *History of Greece* (1846–1856) that fully succeeded in the long run in turning Athens from a negative example into a model for admiration, if not necessarily of emulation.[93] Grote showed that the Athenian democracy was neither the tyranny of the poor, nor the rule of the mob. On the contrary, he argued that only a political system which gave the vote to every citizen could expect that the state would not be run by class groups and the citizen would try to identify with the general interest. Instead of relying on the mixed constitution to achieve this aim, Grote argued that general enfranchisement could end in creating a constitutional morality which would guarantee the stability and success of the system.

There is one final reason why the right to elect the rulers came to be seen as the quintessence of democracy. Following Rousseau, democracy came to be associated with popular sovereignty instead of popular participation in the exercise of power. We have seen how, in antiquity, democracy was identified with the use of the lot in the selection of magistrates, while election was thought to be the characteristic par excellence of oligarchies. This identification was still made until the late eighteenth century: it can still be found in Montesquieu and Rousseau.[94] Until then, election and lot were alternative methods of distributing power among citizens; but once democracy stopped being associated with the sharing of power, and became identified with the popular legitimisation of legislation and government, the properties of lot and election changed radically. Election could now be seen as essential for the popular legitimisation of the laws and the government; from this perspective, the lot had nothing to offer.[95]

Thus, in the period that extended from the American Revolution to the end of World War II, democracy became dissociated from its ancient frame of reference. It was not anymore only one of the many possible ways in which political rule could be organised in a polity: it became the only possible political system in an egalitarian society. Furthermore, democracy ceased to be part of a circle of political change. The association of democracy with a new kind of society gave it a stable and permanent basis: it would not anymore be seen as a political system prone to collapse and transformation into another regime due to its own inherent contradictions. The newly-established link between democracy and popular sovereignty brought a further change: democracy now became the only legitimate political system. It was not anymore a system of sharing power through selection by lot and participation in the assembly, but a form of legitimising power through the election of the rulers. But this dissociation of democracy from its ancient frame of reference was accomplished through the use of alternative conceptions of democracy that originated in antiquity.

We have seen how the ancient Greeks raised the question of who should rule and devised a vocabulary to describe the various forms of political rule. We have followed the afterlife of this vocabulary and the various answers that have been given to this question up to the present day. We have noted the paradox that, although democracy and the vocabulary of constitutions was a Greek invention, modern reflections and transformations of this vocabulary were often based on the image and the history of Rome. Hence, it is not surprising that the leading modern historian of Athenian democracy has found little trace of Athenian democracy functioning as a model during the establishment of modern democracies in the late eighteenth and nineteenth centuries.[96] As we have seen, the Athenian invention of democracy has had a more indirect and complicated influence on modernity. We have also explored how ancient terms and ideas have been developed and transformed in the process of their adoption in the modern world. We should nevertheless finish this chapter on a different note. The ancient answers to the question of who should rule are not important merely because they are the ancestors of our own. They are also important because they open up possibilities which are still untapped.

We have seen above how, during the Hellenistic period, the word democracy came to denote little more than any form of constitution which was not a monarchy. This is strikingly similar to the way democracy has become the only term to describe a non-dictatorial government since World War II. Of course, different people mean different things when they refer to democracy. The ensuing incomprehension is usually solved by adopting an adjective that specifies which version of democracy one has in mind: representative, direct, liberal, totalitarian, radical, proletarian, etc. Enough has already been said about the variety of ancient definitions of democracy to show that no vision of democracy can be considered as the original or the real one. There is a good reason, beyond mere propaganda, for which the most diverse people lay claim to the very same word. The reason is the inherent contradictions of democracy and any other political regime. This allows different people to support and defend different facets of this contradictory form.

Ancient political theory had two great advantages in this respect. It was able to spot the contradictions and even present a mechanism that explained the transformation of one regime into another based on these very contradictions. I am not of course suggesting that there is value in bringing back to life Polybius's cycle of constitutional change as a means of understanding our political present. But we no longer have a way of looking at our political systems and understanding the ways in which they change, collapse and reform; we no longer have a way of looking at democracies in a dynamic and not an essentialist way. When searching for explanations of e.g. the collapse of democratic systems in interwar Europe, we tend to adopt economic or social explanations, for lack of political ones. Finally, the modern abandonment of the ancient question of who should rule is not altogether defensible. Ancient political thought recognised the existence of different individuals, groups and classes in every community and raised the question, which of them should and indeed did hold power? With the significant exception of Marxism, contemporary political thought has largely abandoned both the recognition and the question. The platitudes about popular sovereignty in modern democracies often merely highlight the unwillingness of mainstream contemporary political thought to raise the question and deal with the implications of the answer. In this respect, it is probably the case that the Marxist tradition, which still insists on posing and answering the question in its own chosen terms, is the only surviving inheritor of this brand of ancient political thought. Whether it should be the only one, is rather more debatable.

CHAPTER II

THE EXERCISE OF POWER: LIBERTY

The subject of this chapter follows straight from the previous one. We shall explore how the Greeks and Romans created a discourse about the exercise of power and how this discourse has influenced modern debates. Liberty, in its political sense, concerns the ways in which power is exercised within a political community. Perhaps the best way to introduce the many aspects of this issue is to start with a flashback. In 1819 Benjamin Constant, a French liberal politician and author, gave a famous speech titled 'The Liberty of Ancients Compared with that of Moderns'. A generation after 1789, Constant argued that the excesses of the revolution and the institution of the Terror by the Jacobins were based on an important misconception. The Terror was the result of the misconceived wish to restore in modern conditions an ancient form of liberty. The liberty of the ancients, he argued,

> consisted in exercising collectively, but directly, several parts of the complete sovereignty; in deliberating in the public square, over war and peace; in forming alliances with foreign governments; in voting laws, in pronouncing judgements; in examining the accounts, the acts, the stewardship of the magistrates; in calling them to appear in front of the assembled people, in accusing, condemning or absolving them. But if this is what the ancients called liberty, they admitted as compatible with this collective freedom the complete subjection of the individual to the authority of the community.[1]

Modern freedom on the other hand was very different. Constant went on to explain not only what this modern freedom consisted of, but also why ancient freedom could no more be realised under modern conditions:

> We can no longer enjoy the liberty of the ancients, which consisted in an active and constant participation in collective power. Our freedom must consist of peaceful enjoyment and private independence. The share which in antiquity everyone held in national sovereignty was by no means an abstract presumption as it is in our own day. The will of each individual had real influence: the exercise of this will was a vivid and repeated pleasure. Consequently the ancients were ready to make many a sacrifice to preserve their political rights and their share in the administration of the state. Everybody, feeling with pride all that his suffrage was worth, found in this awareness of his personal importance a great compensation. This compensation no longer exists for us today. Lost in the multitude, the individual can almost never perceive the influence he exercises. Never does his will impress itself upon the whole; nothing confirms in his eyes his own cooperation. The exercise of political rights, therefore, offers us but a part of the pleasures that the ancients found in it, while at the same time the progress of civilization, the commercial tendency of the age, the communication amongst peoples, have infinitely multiplied and varied the means of personal happiness. It follows that we must be far more attached than the ancients to our individual independence. For the ancients, when they sacrificed that independence to their political rights, sacrificed less to obtain more; while in making the same sacrifice, we would give more to obtain less. The aim of the ancients was the sharing of social power among the citizens of the same fatherland: this is what they called liberty. The aim of the moderns is the enjoyment of security in private pleasures; and they call liberty the guarantees accorded by institutions to these pleasures.[2]

The debate on the different forms of liberty was revived after World War II by political philosopher Isaiah Berlin in a highly influential essay titled 'Two concepts of liberty'.[3] In it he distinguished between positive liberty, or self-mastery, and negative liberty, or freedom from interference. Although his definition of negative liberty is very similar to that of Constant, it is not always realised that Berlin's concept of positive freedom is quite different from Constant's depiction of the liberty of the ancients as the freedom to participate in ruling. [4] Berlin's idea of positive liberty entails that a person is really free only when he has managed to master his lower self and liberate his higher self in wishing what he truly wants.[5] Ever since Constant's speech, the subject of ancient vs. modern liberty has retained its fascination. We shall thus explore how the Greeks and Romans invented the concept of liberty as a political value and the many different ways in which it was understood and applied. We shall then look at how these concepts of liberty were revived in modern times and how alternative conceptions of liberty were created in a process of dialogue and opposition.

When we try to understand the conception of liberty in the ancient world we are at a disadvantage. The proclamation of the Universal Declaration of Human Rights in 1948 by the UN finally abolished slavery in its legal form from the whole planet. Therefore, we have no condition to think of as the alternative of liberty. Nothing could be further from the truth when it comes to antiquity. Liberty was originally the condition and status of those people who were not slaves. Since most human societies have employed slaves, the distinction between freedom and slavery has existed in most of them, although relatively few have expressed this distinction as a clear polarity between two incompatible statuses with nothing in between. Nevertheless, since the distinction concerns personal, legal and social status there is no inherent reason for which freedom should become a political concept and value. In fact, most historical societies did not take the step of transferring freedom from the legal and social level to the political field.

In Greek thought a slave was somebody who was under the domination of somebody else and did not have control over his own person.[6] Slavery could thus be contrasted in two different ways. On the one hand, a slave could be contrasted with a master, a person who had power over a slave. On the other hand, the contrast could be with a freeman, somebody who had control over himself and was under the power of nobody else. Naturally, the two different contrasts could become assimilated under certain circumstances. A crucial point came in the early sixth century BCE with the work of Solon. Solon was elected as lawgiver by the Athenians in very troubled circumstances, characterised by intense feuding and deep social rivalries. Many citizens had fallen to slavery through debt; Solon prohibited the enslavement of citizens for debts and thus created a strong link between the status of freedom and citizenship. From now on, the community guaranteed that no citizen could be legally enslaved; the same guarantee did not obviously exist for non-citizens, thus creating a clear dividing line. At the same time the community was ravaged by power struggles among individuals who aimed to establish their own sole rule over it. During the archaic period, many such individuals, called tyrants, overthrew the normal aristocratic regimes and concentrated power in their hands. This monopoly of power by individuals, who treated the rest as inferiors and subordinates, soon came to be seen as the equivalent of a master's rule over his slaves. Solon was the first to describe tyranny as political slavery, thus bringing slavery into the political field.[7]

This process was further accelerated during the Persian Wars (490–479 BCE), when the Greeks successfully resisted against all odds the attempt of the Persian Empire to conquer them. The Greeks saw their struggle as a fight to secure their freedom from Persian domination. Thus, freedom was transferred from a description of personal status to the condition of the community at large. Furthermore, the Greeks attributed their miraculous victory to freedom itself. It was the great political differences between Greek polities and the Persian monarchy which explained why the Greeks could successfully defend the external freedom of their communities. The Persian Empire was seen as the tyranny of a despot who ruled autocratically over slavish subjects; thus, the concept of tyranny as political slavery was now transferred to describe oriental monarchies. On the contrary, the

Greeks were able to fight valiantly, because they were not ruled like slaves, but were free citizens who cared for the good of their communities.[8]

But what exactly did it mean that Greek citizens were free? Because of a lack of sources, it is difficult to say much for any Greek community apart from Athens. In addition, it seems that freedom as a political slogan was particularly associated with democracies, while oligarchs had little use for it.[9] The Athenian conception of freedom joined together a number of themes. Primarily, freedom was the absence of domination, the defining mark of slavery. In order to live without domination, the necessary precondition was to live in a community which was itself free. If the community is under the power of another community or an individual, like a foreign king or dynast, then the citizens cannot decide according to their own will, but everybody can and will be dominated by the arbitrary will of the foreign rulers. Thus, one can be free only in a self-governing community which has its own will. But a self-governing community is no guarantee of freedom, if it is governed in a tyrannical manner. If power is concentrated in the hands of a king or tyrant, or indeed even to a restricted group of citizens, then they would be able to dominate the rest of the citizens and thus freedom would be again extinguished. This idea can be expressed in a number of different ways. The one is to stress that the citizens are not under the whims of their rulers, but live under laws and rules which they themselves have approved. Thus, the rule of law, instead of the arbitrary rule of men, can be one way in which this concept of freedom as non-domination can be expressed. The Athenian orator Demosthenes stated simply that 'no man living will attribute the prosperity of the polis, its democracy and freedom to anything rather than the laws';[10] and his contemporary Hypereides explained:

> Living in a democratic state where justice is established by the laws is different from passing into the power of one tyrant where the caprice of an individual is supreme. We have either to put our trust in laws and so remember freedom or else to be surrendered to the power of one man and brood daily over slavery.[11]

On the other hand, a free person is somebody, who, unlike a slave, does not live under the will of another person. Therefore, another key aspect of freedom was the ability of each citizen to live as one wished. This aspect, which could be seen as the direct ancient analogy to Constant's concept of modern freedom, was constantly praised by partisans of Athenian democracy.[12] As Pericles put it famously in his *Funeral Speech*,

> We live freely concerning both the public realm, and concerning the [lack of] suspicion towards others in their daily pursuits. We do not get into a state with our next-door neighbour if he enjoys himself in his own way, nor do we give him the kind of black looks which, though they do no real harm, still do hurt people's feelings. We are free and tolerant in our private lives; but in public affairs we keep to the law.[13]

Finally, one could stress the equality of participation in power as the guarantee that no citizen is dominated by somebody else. This combination of themes is brought together in a remarkable passage of Aristotle's *Politics*:

> Now a fundamental principle of the democratic form of constitution is liberty – that is what is usually asserted, implying that only under this constitution do men participate in liberty, for they assert this as the aim of every democracy. But one factor of liberty is to govern and be governed in turn ... for they say that each of the citizens ought to have an equal share... This then is one mark of liberty which all democrats set down as a principle of the constitution. And another is for a man to live as he likes; for they say that this is the function of liberty, inasmuch as to live not as one likes is the life of a man that is a slave. This is the second principle of democracy, and from it has come the claim not to be governed, preferably not by anybody, or, failing that, to govern and be governed in turns; and this is the way in which the second principle contributes to equalitarian liberty.[14]

This way of conceptualising freedom had a number of consequences. The first was that freedom entails obligations.[15] Freedom exists only because the city and its institutions guarantee it; unless citizens support the city and its institutions, it will be impossible to retain their freedom. Thus, citizens are obliged to perform services to their community. The easiest way to see this link is in the necessity of military service in order to defend the community from being enslaved to an outside power.

The second is that this particular way of looking at freedom avoids what for us is a potential clash. The Athenians perceived no clash between the claim that freedom existed in the collective exercise of power and the claim that democracies were particularly tolerant systems, where every citizen could live as he wished. Despite this tolerant claim, there was no theoretical limit to what the people, in their collective capacity, could decide, and there was no constitutional limit that could shield the individual from state interference. In a famous case that created endless discussion from antiquity until now, the Athenians sentenced Socrates to death for not honouring the gods of the city and for corrupting the young. Is this not precisely an example of the precariousness of individual freedom, as freedom of conscience, in Athenian democracy?

We tend to distinguish between the rights of the individual and the claims of the state, and we conceive a potential clash between them. Modern liberalism was founded on the principle that the rights of the individual must be protected against the encroachment of the state, otherwise liberty is endangered. But such an argument could not be made in Athens, for the Greeks lacked our concept of rights, which an individual possesses prior to and apart from membership in a human community.[16]

We have already remarked above that, from the time of Solon's reforms, a strong link existed between freedom and citizenship. Citizenship was in fact the guarantee of freedom: a citizen could not be enslaved legally, but the same did not hold true for non-citizens. This link shows why personal freedom was predicated on communal citizenship. To put in the starkest terms, if a Greek city was conquered by its enemies, the free citizen could often find himself sold into slavery. His freedom depended on the freedom and security of his community in the most literal sense.

This is the reason that personal freedom could not be used against the claims of the community: freedom existed only through and within the community. This implied that the freedom of the citizen could only be secured through the performance of civic obligations. The process was reciprocal. What to us appear as individual rights were considered by the Athenians as the results of obligations.[17] The prohibition of summary execution without trial, or the privacy of the house, which we would construe as civic rights, in the eyes of Athenians were seen as the result of the obligations of citizens towards each other and of the community towards its members. Thus, Athenian democracy could show a remarkable degree of tolerance by contemporary standards; but the moment an act, a form of behaviour, or an idea put at jeopardy the safety and liberty of the community, the community had every right and even the obligation to control it or suppress it.[18] Socrates was convicted not because Athenian democracy was keen on intervening in private behaviour or regulating religious beliefs, but because his behaviour had threatened the community by bringing the wrath of the gods and by corrupting the youth. Thus, equality in political participation ensured that nobody would attempt to dominate citizens and threaten their lives, property and security, while at the same time guaranteeing that there would be intervention in citizens' affairs only when the community could agree that there was a threat to its liberty and security.

This democratic defence of liberty encountered many opponents among ancient Greek thinkers. The most important of them was Plato, who, in a memorable passage in the *Republic*, satirically argued that even animals were indeed freer in a democracy.

And the climax of popular liberty, my friend . . . is attained in such a city when the purchased slaves, male and female, are no less free than the owners who paid for them. And I almost forgot to mention the spirit of freedom and equal rights in the relation of men to women and women to men . . . Without experience of it, no-one would believe how much freer the very beasts subject to men are in such a city than elsewhere. The dogs literally verify the adage and 'like their mistresses become'. And, likewise, the horses and asses are wont to hold on their way with the utmost freedom and dignity, bumping into everyone who meets them and who does not step aside. And so, all things everywhere are just bursting with the spirit of liberty.[19]

For Plato, democratic freedom was little more than license and anarchy. This critique led Plato to offer a new conception of freedom. According to Plato, the freedom to live as one wishes is harmful and deceitful for people who are not truly masters of themselves. Our freedom of action is illusory, when we are acting under the compulsion of our desires and passions. A drug addict may appear to be free, but he is actually the slave of his passions, which dominate him and dictate to him what to do. Only when a person has managed to subordinate his desires and passions to the rule of reason can he be truly deemed free.[20] This is the very conception that Isaiah Berlin described as the positive conception of freedom. We see once more how the opposition between freedom and slavery/domination provides the groundwork for a novel conceptualisation; but we also see that the concept of positive freedom was born in explicit opposition to democratic freedom.

The Roman concept of *libertas* shared many features with the Athenian concept of *eleutheria*, while also diverging in important ways.[21] It too had a conception of freedom which was constructed in opposition to slavery. We can also find the theme of liberty as the rule of law instead of men. There is finally to be found the idea that any community where power is concentrated in the hands of an unaccountable ruler loses its liberty. This idea became particularly important in the last century of the Roman republic, when the traditional annual and collegial sharing of power among the elite came under threat from powerful generals, who sought, and ultimately managed, to achieve sole rule. Thus, *libertas* could be used as a cry against the novel threat to the self-governed community. These two issues are nicely brought together by the historian Livy in a passage that would be much quoted by the moderns: 'Henceforward I am to treat of the affairs, civil and military, of a free people, for such the Romans were now become; of annual magistrates and the authority of the laws exalted above that of men'.[22]

To come to differences, *libertas* was never associated with political equality among the citizens in ruling their community.[23] This Athenian conception of freedom could never be adopted in a political system with marked inequalities in the exercise of power. But the biggest difference, and one which would be of immense importance later, was the view of *libertas* as the protection of the individual citizen against the abuse of the power of magistrates. This idea originated in the struggle of the orders between the patricians and the plebeians during the archaic period.[24] The emergence during this struggle of the tribunes, the plebeian officers whose task was to protect the plebeians against the patrician magistrates, was seen as the crucial element for the preservation of freedom for the lower classes. This was effected through the processes of *provocatio*, the right of every citizen to appeal to the Roman people as the ultimate judge, and *auxilium*, in which, if a magistrate attempted to use his official power against a citizen, the citizen could ask for the intervention of a tribune, who could rescue the citizen and forbid the magistrate to carry out his decision until the tribune himself had decided on the case. Livy famously called the aid of the tribunes (*auxilium*) and the right of appeal to the Roman plebs (*provocatio*) as 'the two bulwarks of Roman liberty'.[25] Thus, this Roman conception of freedom could be enshrined in particular laws and institutions; but, even more, it could be approached from the perspective of the individual citizen. As we shall see, this fact would be of enormous importance for the emergence of the language of natural rights in early modern Europe. Thus, in contrast to Athens, where the concept of freedom referred to the community as a whole and its collective exercise of power, in Rome, freedom could be seen from the perspective of the individual citizen and his protection from the abuse of power by the authorities.

There is one last element of ancient conceptions of liberty we need to look at. This is the connection between freedom and power over others. We saw earlier that slaves could be juxtaposed to freemen, but also to masters; not all freemen were masters of course, but it was relatively easy to make the connection and argue that the free par excellence were those who could exercise power over others. And already in the work of Herodotus we encounter the idea that a free community will be able to rule over others.

> Thus, Athens went from strength to strength, and proved, if proof were needed, how noble a thing equality of speech is, not in one respect only, but in all; for while they were oppressed under tyrants, they had no better success in war than any of their neighbours, yet, once the yoke was flung off, they proved the finest fighters in the world. This clearly shows that, so long as they were held down by authority, they deliberately shirked their duty in the field, as slaves shirk working for their masters; but when freedom was won, then every man amongst them was interested in his own cause.[26]

Freedom, in giving every citizen an incentive for caring for his community and its preservation, made free communities invincible in war and offered them the opportunity to rule over others. In fact, the Athenian Empire was precisely seen as rule gained in the struggle for freedom and as making the Athenians the freest community.[27] But this discourse of liberty and empire created a paradox. Success in war and in creating an empire could ultimately lead to the very loss of liberty that was the initial spur to the creation of empire. Herodotus has Cyrus, the king who created the Persian Empire, advising the Persians against moving from their barren mountains into the fertile plains in order to reap the benefits of empire, because that would destroy their frugal and martial spirit and make them slaves instead of rulers.[28]

This set of ideas was taken over and further developed by the Roman historians and thinkers. According to them, the expansion of Roman power was the direct result of the establishment of freedom. As the historian Sallust commented in a famous passage,

At this period every citizen began to seek distinction, and to display his talents with greater freedom; for, with princes, the meritorious are greater objects of suspicion than the undeserving, and to them the worth of others is a source of alarm. But when liberty was secured, it is almost incredible how much the state strengthened itself in a short space of time, so strong a passion for distinction had pervaded it.[29]

So the power and expansion of Rome was due to Roman liberty. But, in the end, the Romans had to face the fate that Cyrus warned the Persians against. If the expansion of Roman power was the result of Roman liberty, the Roman Empire ultimately paved the way for the demise of this very liberty. The generals who received extensive powers and large armies in order to expand the empire ultimately used these armies to subvert the free commonwealth. According to Sallust, the extinction of the *metus hostilis* (fear of the enemy) brought luxury and corruption to Rome and sapped the spirit that was necessary to maintain Roman freedom. The Roman emperors finally sealed the fate of Rome by extinguishing freedom in order to achieve safety and stability. As the Roman historian Tacitus phrased it, 'the Principate and liberty were irreconcilable'.[30]

Modern times

We can summarise the above discussion of ancient discourses on freedom by noting the importance of certain themes: the conception of freedom as the opposite of slavery and tyranny; the link between individual and collective freedom; the relationship between freedom and the performance of obligations; the dialectic between liberty and empire; the connection between freedom as protection and agencies which are able to secure this protection; and, finally, the concept of freedom as self-mastery. All these themes played a significant role in modern debates and discussions.

The revival of the concept of liberty as an essential part of political discourse took place in Italy in the later Middle Ages. The emergence of the Italian city-states led to incessant battles against the Holy Roman Emperor, the Papacy and local *signori* in order to preserve their autonomy and self-government. The rediscovery, during the later Middle Ages, of Roman law and the works of Aristotle played a fundamental role in the construction of a discourse which put liberty as a treasured value of the Italian republics. But the rediscovery and fresh study of classical texts by the humanist scholars during the Renaissance provided contemporary thinkers with a whole new world of concepts and images with which to talk and think about liberty.[31] It was mainly in Florence, the stalwart defender of republican liberty, that most of these new ideas emerged. It was here that Roman history ceased to be seen through the prism of the Empire and became the story of the acquisition and loss of liberty of the Roman republic. This was expressed in a most vivid way when Coluccio Salutati, one of the most important Florentine intellectuals, argued that Florence, the bastion of liberty, was not founded by Julius Caesar, as was thought until then, but by the veterans of Sulla, while Roman freedom was not yet extinguished.[32] The Roman juxtaposition of *regnum* to *libertas* was thus revived to praise and defend liberty from the monarchic threat and to argue for the necessity of a self-governing republic for the preservation of freedom.

It was within this context that another Florentine brought back to life another aspect of ancient discussions of freedom. Machiavelli revived a distinction, first drawn by Polybius, between republics for preservation and republics for expansion.[33] Sparta was the ideal example of the first case and Rome of the second. Confronted with the dilemma of choosing between preservation and expansion, Machiavelli stated his preference for the pursuit of power and empire. The problem with choosing the road of preservation is that it can open the way to the loss of liberty in the hands of an expanding community. Thus, the pursuit of power is the best means to ensure that a republic will not be enslaved itself, and also the best way to achieve glory. Machiavelli was painfully aware of the ancient conclusion that the pursuit of empire can lead to the loss of freedom. But he argued, with reason, that a polity for preservation might be forced to pursue expansion against its will or else inaction would enervate its military spirit; thus, it is preferable to opt for expansion and glory in the first place.[34] Machiavelli launched an exploration of the relationship between liberty and empire which lasted until well into the eighteenth century.[35]

But how is a community to achieve glory and empire? Machiavelli stressed anew the connection between liberty and empire that was posited by ancient texts:

> It is easy to see how this affection of peoples for self-government comes about, for experience shows that cities have never increased in dominion or wealth unless they have been independent. It is truly remarkable to observe the greatness which Athens attained in the space of a hundred years after it had been liberated from the tyranny of Peisistratus. But most marvellous of all is it to observe the greatness which Rome attained after freeing itself from its kings.[36]

Thus, freedom was necessary in order to achieve success in war and empire. From this Machiavelli drew a novel conclusion. It was necessary for a polity that aspired to empire to include the masses in its function, for without them no expansive army could ever succeed. He argued extensively in favour of citizen militias and against the common contemporary practice of using mercenaries. The Roman citizen-soldiers who created a world empire were Machiavelli's ideal example. In order to incorporate the masses into the function of the polity it was necessary to preserve freedom and to destroy domination of one group by the other. Machiavelli believed that in every community there existed two *humori*: the *grandi*, who want to dominate, and the people, who want not to be dominated but wish to be left alone to pursue their goals. Using Roman history as an illustration, he identified the first group with the patricians and the second with the plebs. Thus, Machiavelli accepted the classical theme that domination was a constant danger in every human community. In his view, the guardianship of liberty should be entrusted to those with no wish to dominate others. Therefore, he again approved of Rome where this power rested with the plebeians and interpreted the emergence of the tribunes as the instrument that guaranteed the preservation of the freedom of the masses. Machiavelli's discussion of freedom was mainly geared towards the issue of liberty and empire; but through the implications of this concern he also came to think about freedom as the protection of the masses from their rulers.

Machiavelli's discussion of freedom had a tremendous influence on later discussions. While the early Renaissance was a period in which the Italian city-states managed to flourish and develop a discourse of republican freedom, the sixteenth century signalled an opposite trend that lasted until the French Revolution. In most European countries the monarchs initiated a process of concentrating power in their own hands through the means of taxation and warfare, and they often managed to bypass the resistance of the various estates, cities and orders that until then had shared power to a significant extent. This process did not occur without resistance and did not happen with the same intensity or speed in all countries. What is of importance here is that the ancient discourses on freedom played an immensely important role in providing those who resisted the rise of absolutism with a language of defence and an image of an alternative. In certain favourable circumstances, as we shall see, it was possible to use the language of free states in order to portray and construct an alternative to monarchy and absolutist government. But, for most of the time, it was the concept of freedom as protection that was highly important for resisting the claims of absolutism.

Thus, during the sixteenth century it was primarily the image of the Roman tribunes and the Spartan ephors as means of resistance to tyranny and protection of freedom that captivated the minds of contemporaries. The religious wars between Catholics and Protestants were the dominant feature of that century in most European countries. The situation was further complicated by the fact that in both England and France the monarchy was directly implicated in these conflicts by supporting one side against the other; a further complication was that in both countries the monarchy alternated between supporting one faith against the other. It was, therefore, highly relevant for both Catholics and Protestants that they could justify resistance to a monarch, not on religious grounds, but by invoking the language of freedom and slavery and by pinpointing an institution which could act as the protector and guarantor of the freedom of citizens.

How could resistance to authority be justified and who should resist? Contemporaries tried to answer the first question by recourse to the idea of a covenant between the ruler and the ruled.[37] This covenant specified the rights and obligations of both, and, in the event that it was undermined by the ruler, provided the justification for resisting his authority. In this respect, the Spartan institution of the ephors provided an excellent analogy that was much employed. The ephors and the Spartan kings exchanged oaths every month, in which the kings promised to observe the laws and the ephors to uphold their authority if they did so. This oath exchange was seen as a model for the contractual relationship between modern rulers and their subjects.[38] But who should resist the tyrannical authority? The problem here was that a general right to resistance would be impossible to differentiate from rebellion, anarchy or homicide. Thus it was necessary to entrust specific institutions or lesser magistracies with the task of protecting the freedoms of the citizens and resisting the authorities. The Roman plebeian conception of freedom was of particular importance in this respect: it justified specific liberties, enshrined in specific laws and protected by specific agencies. The Roman tribunate was particularly influential in early modern attempts to locate an institution that could be entrusted with the protection of citizens' freedoms and resistance to unlawful authorities.[39]

But, in other circumstances, it was possible to move further ahead and put Machiavelli's reformulation of ancient freedom to novel uses. The catalyst for this development was the English civil war (1640–1651), which pitted Charles I against the Parliament. Many supporters of the parliamentarian cause chose to argue that the royal prerogative of vetoing parliament's laws was a mark of slavery on the English commonwealth. To live under the will of an individual, even if he chose not to exercise this will, destroyed the freedom of the English citizens. The civil war was thus seen as the inevitable result of the king's attempt to enforce his prerogative, thereby robbing his subjects of their liberty.[40] In contrast, the language of liberty could be used to defend the new republican regime that followed the execution of the king.

This view of liberty was directly challenged for the first time from a modern perspective by Thomas Hobbes, in his famous masterpiece, the *Leviathan* (1651). According to Hobbes, it was the readings of ancient texts that made his contemporaries conceive of liberty as the opposite of monarchy and domination. It is worth quoting this passage at length:

> In these western parts of the world, we are made to receive our opinions concerning the institution, and rights of commonwealths, from Aristotle, Cicero, and other men, Greeks and Romans . . . And because the Athenians were taught, to keep them from desire of changing their government, that they were freemen, and all that lived under monarchy were slaves; therefore Aristotle puts it down in his *Politics*. '*In democracy, liberty is to be supposed: for it is commonly held, that no man is free in any other government.*' And as Aristotle; so Cicero, and other writers have grounded their civil doctrine on the opinions of the Romans, who were taught to hate monarchy, at first, by them that, having deposed their sovereign, shared amongst them the sovereignty of Rome; and afterwards by their successors. And by reading of these Greek and Latin authors, men from their childhood have gotten a habit, under a false show of liberty, of favouring tumults and of licentiouly controlling the actions of their sovereigns and again of controlling those controllers; with the effusion of so much blood, as I think I may truly say, there was never any thing so dearly bought as these western parts have bought the learning of the Greek and Latin tongues.[41]

Hobbes proposed a very different definition of freedom, which has remained a dominant way of thinking about freedom ever since.[42] Freedom, in this view, is the lack of interference. To the extent that somebody is not actively constrained by law to act in a certain way, then one is to be considered free. Therefore, the famous liberty of the ancients had very specious claims to modern admiration:

> The liberty, whereof there is so frequent and honourable mention in the histories and philosophy of the ancient Greeks and Romans, and in the writings and discourse of those that from them have received all their learning in politics, is not the liberty of particular men but the liberty of the commonwealth: which is the same as that which every man would have if there were no civil laws or commonwealth at all . . . The Athenians and Romans were free; that is free commonwealths; no particular men had the liberty to resist their own representative, but their representative had the liberty to resist or invade other people. There is, to this day, written in great characters on the turrets of the city of Lucca, the word *libertas*. Yet no-one can infer that a particular man has more liberty, or immunity from the service of the commonwealth, there than in Constantinople. Whether a commonwealth be monarchical or popular, the freedom is still the same.[43]

Thus, in an impressive move against the ancients, Hobbes had managed to turn the tables. Liberty should not anymore be sought in the external freedom of the community or the political freedom of participating in government. Instead, under the most different political systems, from absolutism to direct democracy, freedom should be sought in the extent to which an individual is left without interference from the community. An absolute monarchy which did not interfere with the lives of its subjects was far freer than a direct democracy which constantly interfered through legislation. In this way, Hobbes attempted to counter the theory that in a monarchy all citizens were slaves under the arbitrary will of the ruler. Thus, Constant's modern liberty and Berlin's negative liberty were first articulated by Hobbes in an explicit contrast with ancient political thought.

While proposing a new conception of freedom, Hobbes also brought in a new language of political theory. This was the language of natural rights. We have seen that no arguments based on rights existed in antiquity. But it was, nevertheless, an ancient language which provided medieval and early modern Europeans with the means of discussing natural rights. This was the language of Roman law.[44] Roman law, as codified under the emperors, displayed a strong interest in the regulation of issues relating to property and had developed a complex structure of concepts and practices, which were elaborated by a long jurisprudential tradition. Roman law had construed property as *dominium*, that which pertained to the master (*dominus*); thus, the absolute power of a master over his slaves provided the model of conceiving property as absolute and indivisible. On the other hand, the Romans had developed the concept of *ius*, which we can roughly translate as right. As a result of this conception, the *Digest*, the most important codification of Roman law, could define justice as 'the constant and perpetual aim of giving each person his own right, *ius suum*'.[45]

The concepts of *ius* and *dominium* were only relevant to Roman private law; but they could potentially be taken from the private context and employed to describe relationships in the public sphere between the citizens and the community, between the ruler and the subjects and between the citizens themselves.[46] When Roman law was rediscovered and re-employed during the Middle Ages, it provided thinkers with a language and a number of concepts which would fundamentally shape the course of Western political thought up to the present day.[47] In classical Roman law, property and right had remained two separate concepts. But, when Roman law was rediscovered and re-employed during the Middle Ages, there started a process which ultimately led to the conflation between the two concepts.[48] The crucial point was seemingly reached during a theological controversy revolving around the refusal of the Franciscan monastic order to hold any property. It was during this controversy that right was identified as an individual's property in the same absolute manner that one possessed a piece of property; and it was in the aftermath of this controversy that property came to seen widely as a right of the individual person. Finally, a further twist delivered the concept of natural rights: rights that the law of nature decreed as inherent to the individual person.

Hobbes made an important contribution to this tradition by joining freedom with the concept of natural rights. For Hobbes, freedom was the condition of man in the state of nature, the condition of human beings before entering human communities. This was a radically egalitarian and individualist vision of human beings. In this original state, all humans were equal and possessed the same natural rights to self-preservation which derive from the law of nature. But precisely because of their equality, according to Hobbes, there ensued a perpetual state of war, since no human was superior enough to be able to subjugate the others. The only solution to perpetual war and anarchy was the creation of a covenant by which everybody surrendered his natural freedom to a sovereign, whose purpose was to guarantee the preservation of the natural rights of the subjects through the force of law. While Hobbes argued that natural rights should be surrendered in exchange for the protection and freedom offered by the sovereign, later thinkers, like John Locke, argued that property and freedom of conscience were inalienable rights of human beings, whose protection is the purpose of the formation of political communities. In this complex way, Roman law had provided early modern thinkers with the concepts for constructing a theory of freedom in which citizens could defend their inalienable natural rights against the claims of the state and its rulers.[49]

Hobbes's views were not left without answer; in these answers we can see a complex process of adoption and negation that led to an ultimate transformation of the ancient conceptions of freedom. The first restatement of ancient freedom, which also bears traces of the influence of Hobbes, was Marchamont Nedham's *The Excellencie of a Free State* (1656). The title of the work testifies to the adoption of the ancient argument that only in a free state, which is not dominated externally or internally, can freedom exist.[50] Nedham presented eloquently the advantages of a free state, which is not dominated by a king or a senatorial aristocracy, with Rome acting as the major historical example. Liberty is the chief outcome of such a free state and Nedham saw liberty from two different perspectives. On the one hand, he restated the ancient connection between liberty and empire, arguing that only a free state can defend the freedom of the community from external enemies and extend its power. In fact, he contrasted the military successes of the new republic in Scotland, Ireland and the Caribbean with English impotence under the kings as evidence of this link between freedom, glory and power.[51] But Nedham believed that republican freedom could be justified on other grounds as well.

> As the end of all government is (or ought to be) the good and ease of the people, in a secure enjoyment of their rights, without pressure and oppression: so questionless the people, who are most sensible of their own burthens, being once put into a capacity and freedom of acting, are the most likely to provide remedies for their own relief; they only know where the shoe wrings.[52]

Thus, Nedham was able to employ the language of rights and, at the same time, insist that only where people rule themselves can they protect their rights. This was an important development because later thinkers would come to repudiate Nedham's first defence of liberty, as the means to empire and glory, and emphasise the second.

After the Restoration of the Stuart monarchy in 1660, the ancient discourses on freedom and the modern language of rights shaped a language of opposition that played a fundamental role in eighteenth-century British history. This opposition was centred initially on the Whigs who aimed to exclude James II from acceding to the throne; after the Glorious Revolution of 1688 they re-emerged as the Country or Independent Whigs, to differentiate them from the Court Whigs who held power during most of the eighteenth century. These thinkers abandoned the premise that monarchy was tantamount to arbitrary power and slavery; a limited monarchy could be compatible with liberty. Instead, they shifted the discussion of tyranny and liberty to a new context. The context of this novel employment of the language of liberty was what many contemporaries considered as an attempt of the monarchy to overthrow the ancient constitution and substitute it with arbitrary government. The monarchy had not attempted a direct confrontation with the parliament, like in the era before the Civil War; instead, it had used other means to effect a real concentration of power, while the constitutional veneer would remain the same.[53] The opposition decried in particular two practices: the use of corruption and the standing army.

The British crown and its government had managed to perfect the game of patronage and influence. By appointments to lucrative posts, by perquisites and by pensions it had managed to secure a stable and docile majority in the parliament which frustrated every attempt of the Country opposition. The opposition defined these policies as corruption that posed a direct threat to the preservation of liberty. In order to be able to defend their freedom, citizens would have to be independent. Otherwise, they would be under the power and influence of the rulers and would become either impotent or tools in their hands. Landed property provided the best means to independence and this school of thought retained a strong preference for independent farmers as the foundation of a free community. This explains why the opposition chose to present the conflict as one between Country and the Court.

In this respect, there was no better source of appeal than the overthrow of the Roman republic by Augustus and the history of the Roman emperors. While the British eighteenth century is known as the Augustan age, it should be stressed that for many contemporaries Augustus was an odious figure.[54] Tacitus was the author of choice for those who wanted to criticise the growing demise of freedom and to study the machinations of courts to exterminate liberty. He provided the opposition authors with a deep mistrust of the rulers and the constant need for vigilance against them. Two of the most influential political works of these opposition authors were an edition of the works of Tacitus (1737) with extensive commentary by Thomas Gordon[55] and *Cato's Letters* (1724) by Gordon and John Trenchard.[56] The opposition often used the image of Rome under the emperors, where the façade had remained the same and the people went on to elect tribunes and consuls, while in reality the emperors wielded uncontested power and strangled freedom, in order to warn about the dangers ahead.[57]

This theme was closely linked with the second issue: standing armies. England had been an exception to the common European standard of a monarchy employing a standing army, mainly due to her insular position and the fact that the parliament controlled the taxation necessary to fund one. But, after the Glorious Revolution, the monarchy managed to maintain a standing army on a permanent basis with the assent of a collaborative parliament. This standing army was a direct threat to liberty, the opposition writers argued, and Roman history provided them with a paradigmatic case of the threat at hand. As long as Rome was based on a citizen militia, it was possible both to maintain freedom and to excel in war. But as soon as Marius, at the beginning of the first century BCE, transformed the Roman militia into a professional army, the road to the loss of liberty, finally achieved by Caesar and Augustus, was open. For these opposition authors the Roman emperors were little more than arbitrary rulers based on a standing army. Again, the independence of the citizen, best achieved through the possession of land, was necessary for the creation of a militia and the avoidance of a standing army.

The Country or Independent Whigs created a political discourse which fused the modern language of natural rights with the Roman conception of freedom and the lessons of Roman history. The central element of this political discourse was the fear of power and the belief that the rulers were constantly conspiring to overthrow the liberty of the subjects and to enslave them. The keyword of this opposition language was vigilance. If citizens wanted to ensure that their freedom was not destroyed by their rulers, they had to be constantly vigilant of the government's schemes and plans. This language ultimately crossed the Atlantic and provided the colonists with the means for resisting British rule and justifying the American Revolution of 1776.[58] The leaders of the American Revolution could appeal at the same time to 'Aristotle and Plato, Livy and Cicero, and Sidney, Harrington and Locke'[59] for the principles of liberty, without thus feeling any contradiction. Roman history and the Roman heroes of Livy and Plutarch were used not only as models in the fight for freedom, but also as warnings about the dangers corruption and arbitrary rule posed to it.[60] The opposition to standing armies and the valorisation of citizen militias was ultimately enshrined in the Second Amendment of the American Constitution, which specifies that a militia and the right of the people to bear arms shall not be infringed. In this respect it is a direct legacy of an ancient discourse.

Thus, one of the currents that fed into the liberal tradition placed an important value on antiquity and ancient political thought. Roman history was of particular importance in exemplifying the dangers that threatened liberty, castigating the tyranny of arbitrary rule and expressing an inherent distrust of power. It is true that, within this current, antiquity was more often used as a means of criticising modern phenomena than as a positive model; but it was also possible to use antiquity in order to endorse the rule of law or to present Cato or Cicero as models of freedom fighters.

Another current that ultimately became part of the liberal tradition was created in explicit opposition to ancient politics and political thought. The distinction between the two conceptions of freedom drawn by Hobbes in the seventeenth century acquired a new meaning during the eighteenth. It now became part of a discussion about two widely divergent views of human community. The liberty of the ancients came to be seen as the expression of a certain kind of society; and the new conception of freedom came to be seen as the characteristic trait of modern European societies. Thus, antiquity and ancient freedom became pieces of contention in a battle about the nature and future of European societies.

The opening salvo in this debate was effectively the work of Montesquieu. Montesquieu brought together two of the main themes in the discussion of liberty. The relationship between liberty and empire was the subject of his *Considerations on the Causes of the Greatness and Decline of the Romans* (1734). Montesquieu sought to debunk the myth of Roman power by presenting Rome as a place devoid of arts and commerce, whose inhabitants had recourse only to pillage in order to enrich themselves. For Montesquieu, Roman power and expansion was not the result of Roman liberty; rather, it was the result of a primitive economy and a political system which channelled internal feuds into external aggression. The Roman glory and power had few merits in his eyes; the despotism of the emperors was only the natural result of a quest for power that had little to recommend it.[61]

Montesquieu also denied strongly the connection between self-government and freedom that modern thinkers had adopted from the Greeks and Romans:

> Liberty is a right of doing whatever the laws permit . . . Democracy and aristocracy are not free states by their nature. Political liberty is to be found only in moderate governments. But it is not always in moderate states. It is present only when power is not abused, but it has eternally been observed that any man who has power is led to abuse it, he continues until he finds limits . . . So that one cannot abuse power, power must check power by the arrangement of things. A constitution can be such that no-one will be constrained to do the things that the law does not oblige him to do, or be kept from doing the things that the law permits him to do.[62]

Montesquieu shed the connection between freedom and political regime with its ancient pedigree; as long as there is division of power between different bodies which are able to mutually check each other, the form of political regime has no bearing on the extent of liberty enjoyed by the citizens. For Montesquieu, freedom was the rule of law. The preservation of freedom could only be secured through an institutional mechanism that ensured that people were not under the arbitrary power of their rulers, but that everything would be regulated by rules applying to everybody. He thus drew a distinction between legislative, executive and judicial power and argued that modern England, not an ancient republic, was the country which enjoyed freedom par excellence, because there the three powers were distinguished and balanced.[63]

Montesquieu created the setting for a new discussion of ancient and modern freedom.[64] This distinction was one of the most contested issues during the French Enlightenment.[65] While there was no such extensive debate in Britain, the subject exercised the most significant representatives of the Scottish Enlightenment, such as David Hume, Adam Ferguson and Adam Smith.[66] According to the opponents of ancient freedom, antiquity was characterised by small polities, overwhelmingly based on agriculture and constantly at each other's throat. In these societies the main way of enrichment lay in warfare. The booty acquired, the territory conquered and the slaves captured explained why ancient citizens were so keen to participate in war. Failing to defend the community adequately could end up in the loss of crops and land to an invading army, but also in enslavement and destruction; ancient liberty was the spirit necessary for the preservation of ancient polities in a world of constant warfare. On the other hand, success in war could bring enormous power and wealth. Not only was it the only way of significant enrichment in primitive ancient economies, but the thousands of captive slaves could be used to alleviate citizens from the need to work to make a living. Thus, because of the subordination of slaves, the citizens were able to devote their time to public affairs and the defence of the freedom of their community. The loudest exaltations of citizen freedom in antiquity went hand in hand with the cruellest treatment of all those unfortunate human beings who had to perform the necessary menial tasks. The freedom of the citizen was bought at the price of the enslavement of a large section of ancient societies.

> This last was the station, which, in the distinction betwixt freemen and slaves, the citizens of every ancient republic strove to gain, and to maintain for themselves . . . In this manner, the honours of one half of the species were sacrificed to those of the other; as stones from the same quarry are buried in the foundation, to sustain the blocks which happen to be hewn for the superior parts of the pile. In the midst of our encomiums bestowed on the Greeks and the Romans, we are, by this circumstance, made to remember, that no human institution is perfect . . . We feel its injustice; we suffer for the helot, under the severities and unequal treatment to which he was exposed: but when we think only of the superior order of men in this state; when

we attend to that elevation and magnanimity of spirit, for which danger had no terror, interest no means to corrupt; when we consider them as friends, or as citizens, we are apt to forget, like themselves, that slaves have a title to be treated like men.[67]

On the contrary, historical development had led to modern societies that were radically different. The key concept in these eighteenth-century debates was commerce.[68] Commerce did not only denote trade, but human interaction and exchange in general. The importance of commerce lay in the fact that it enabled a whole spectrum of activities and experiences which were impossible in ancient societies. Commerce made it possible for people to prosper without recourse to militaristic expansion. Even more, it made military expansion in the old manner superfluous, if not actually counter-productive. Modern states derived their wealth and power from trade, and trade required stability and mutual understanding. A state could not surpass another state's commercial wealth through warfare or conquest, as happened in the ancient agricultural states. The expansion of commerce tended to force states to recognise the necessity of stability and the futility of war; in fact, it had created an interconnected system of balance, which made it impossible for any state to achieve the conquest of the other states and create a universal empire like that of Rome. Furthermore, commerce, as eighteenth-century thinkers phrased it, 'polished the manners' through communication and interaction and made the aggressive militaristic spirit of ancient societies even more of an anachronism in the modern world. Finally, commerce created a market in which people exchanged services; it thus made it possible for the lower classes to remain free, while selling their labour, and thereby gave birth to a society without social dependence and slavery. Modern liberty was, or could be, extended to everybody. In modern society the working classes were not slaves anymore, but freemen who could enjoy the security of property and the pursuit of happiness in equal measure with the elite.

The end result of this attack on the ancients was the conclusion that freedom was much more extensive in modern societies, and the denial that freedom had any connection with the form of the polity. David Hume provided a lucid expression of this argument:

> The chief difference between the *domestic* economy of the ancients and that of the moderns consists in the practice of slavery, which prevailed among the former, and which has been abolished for some centuries throughout the greater part of Europe. Some passionate admirers of the ancients, and zealous partisans of civil liberty, (for these sentiments, as they are, both of them, in the main, extremely just, are found to be almost inseparable) cannot forbear regretting the loss of this institution; and, whilst they brand all submission to the government of a single person with the harsh denomination of slavery, they would gladly reduce the greater part of mankind to real slavery and subjection. But, to one who considers coolly on the subject, it will appear that human nature, in general, really enjoys more liberty at present, in the most arbitrary government of Europe, than it ever did during the most flourishing period of ancient times.[69]

But not everybody agreed that this sense of freedom was a great advantage of modern polities. The most influential critic of this line of thought was undoubtedly J. J. Rousseau. The very opening words of his *Social Contract* were 'Man is born free; and everywhere he is in chains'.[70] Rousseau shared with Hobbes and Locke the idea of natural human freedom and equality before the institution of political communities. But he deeply differed from them in arguing that the development of culture, civilisation and technology had made man more unfree than ever. These developments had led to the emergence of inequality and dependence on other human beings; as a result, not only did man depend on other human beings for his subsistence and survival, but also had to rely on other people's beliefs and views to satisfy his psychological needs. The modern man in commercial societies might possess freedom of action in theory, but the society in which he lived had determined beforehand what he could use this freedom for:

The ancient peoples are no longer a model for the modern. They are too foreign in every respect. . . . You are neither Romans nor Spartans; you are not even Athenians. Leave aside these great names that ill suit you. You are merchants, artisans, bourgeois, always occupied with private interest, work, business and gain; people for whom freedom itself is only a means of acquiring without obstacle and possessing with security.[71]

Rousseau was the first modern thinker to argue that social and economic inequality and dependence were as important causes of the undermining of freedom as political inequality and domination. But he was not content with criticising the materialistic and individualistic flavour of modern freedom; he went on to construct an alternative conception of freedom, on which ancient political thought had an enormous influence. Rousseau joined the modern language of the social contract with the ancient concept of freedom as non-domination and the Platonic conception of freedom as rational liberation.[72] Man had lost his natural freedom, which could not be retrieved; his only chance of being free within society was to create a community in which he would only obey the rules he had set down himself. Instead of being dependent on other human beings and their views and wills, man would become free by obeying only the general will, whose ordinances he had participated in defining.[73] Rousseau suggested that the general will should define the laws by which the community would live, and that every citizen should participate in the legislative process which would determine what the general will was. Only personal and direct participation in the formation of the general will could make men free; the modern system of representation was, for Rousseau, nothing more than political slavery.

But in order for the citizens to be able to identify with the general will and the interests of the community instead of their private or sectional interests, it was necessary to construct a community with minimum social and economic inequality. Rousseau did not place much emphasis on this second condition, though it would become enormously important in later times; but his identification of freedom in society with political participation was one of the clearest messages of his work. It was Sparta and Rome which provided Rousseau with images of what his suggested model would look like. Sparta was a community without inequality and without the corrupting influences of civilisation and technology, which bred dependence and domination.[74] This allowed the Spartans to be free by devoting themselves to communal aims they had set themselves, instead of dependence on other human beings. And Rome was a model of how political freedom, as mass citizen participation in setting the laws and determining the general will, could actually function.

Along with Rousseau's novel conception of freedom, the language of opposition forged in Britain found its way to France in the course of the eighteenth century.[75] Thinkers like Mably and Saige[76] managed to combine, in a potent mix, the language of opposition with a radicalised version of natural rights.[77] It was not the primary language used to denounce royal absolutism; but the growing radicalisation of French politics meant that this language would acquire immense influence at the time of the Revolution.

When the Estates General transformed into the National Assembly in June 1789, marking the beginning of the French Revolution, they adopted Rousseau's view of the general will, but with a significant modification. The National Assembly asserted that freedom could only be preserved if every citizen had assented to the laws that he had to obey; and these laws expressed the general will of the nation. But, in contrast to Rousseau, who had argued that only by participating directly in legislative sovereignty could the citizens remain free, the National Assembly moved that it was only the elected representatives of the people who could express the general will of the nation. This opened the path for the criticism that the representatives were only usurpers of the general will and that sovereignty resided only with the people at large. It was at this moment that the language of opposition acquired an immense importance. Its distrust of power, its critique of usurpation, its contrast between liberty and tyranny and its call for vigilance and popular mobilisation to protect liberty were explosive in circumstances of external war and widespread conspiracy and treason by the king and the old elite. It was in this context that the language of opposition mixed with Rousseau's theory of freedom and led to what contemporaries called the Terror.[78]

It was in reaction to the French Revolution and its presumed attempt to revive ancient freedom in modern conditions that Constant wrote his famous speech that we considered at the beginning of this paper.[79] As we can now see, Constant's was the final articulation of a number of debates that had been taking place since Hobbes. Two of its main themes acquired their significance because of the experience of the French Revolution. Constant, and many continental liberals in the nineteenth century and ever since, were profoundly disturbed by the phenomenon of the Terror. An assembly which claimed to represent the people, along with direct political participation in the form of insurrections and demonstrations, had invaded the freedom of the citizens and infringed the rights to life, conscience and property. Accordingly, they were fearful of two theories that were inspired by republican Rome: the earlier Whig urge to popular vigilance against authorities and the new theory of the general will and popular sovereignty. It should be clear by now that what Constant attacked as the liberty of the ancients, was in reality a modern construction based on a significant transformation of ancient elements.

The liberal fear of ancient freedom as political participation had its origins in these circumstances. Only if strict limits to the ability of the community to invade the rights and freedom of the individual were erected could freedom be secured. For this to happen, it was necessary to curb direct political participation by the masses, with its concomitant dangers, along with a division between legislative, executive and judicial power along the lines suggested by Montesquieu. But, more than this, it was necessary to create a clear distinction between the public and the private sphere and to deny the community the right to interfere with people's activities, thoughts and inclinations in their private sphere.[80] For Constant, the modern attempt to revive ancient freedom was both dangerous and conducive to failure: conducive, because freedom as political participation could not have the same value in modern large states; dangerous, because ancient freedom ignored the distinction between private and public and the protection of individual rights. Thus, one tradition of modern liberalism was born in explicit opposition to what it considered the modern revival of ancient liberty; while another, based on vigilance against arbitrary rulers, corruption and standing armies, came to life through the influence of Roman freedom and the example of Roman history.[81]

It is time to reach some conclusions. The modern concept of negative freedom, together with the language of rights, has certainly exercised a very beneficial role in the shaping of the modern world. The eighteenth-century thinkers who attacked the ancients for denying any rights to women or slaves, or for failing to recognise the freedom of consciousness or the right to privacy, had certainly scored an important point. In this respect, negative freedom and the language of rights have certainly helped to create a freer world. It is also the case that the language of rights has a great ability to provide people with a means of articulating claims and demanding their respect. Accordingly, it is likely that the language of rights will remain a dominant force in shaping the way we think about freedom.[82]

Is this evidence that the influence of ancient ideas about freedom belongs to the past and has only historical interest? Is not the existence of slavery in ancient societies a clear case of the anachronistic and hypocritical nature of ancient freedom, as Constant believed? I feel that the case is rather different. Slavery for the Greeks and Romans defined a situation in which an individual or a community was under the power of another individual or community. Seen in this light, slavery was not a legal status that could be abolished by legislative fiat. Slavery was the pragmatic result of the existence of inequality of power and wealth among individuals and communities. From the individual's point of view, slavery was considered either as a form of bad luck, or a necessity for civilised life. There is nothing specifically Greek about this attitude, as the philosopher Bernard Williams argued some time ago:

> The main feature of the Greek attitude to slavery, I have suggested, was not a morally primitive belief in its justice, but the fact that

[considerations of justice and injustice were immobilised by the demands of what was seen as social and economic necessity.] The phenomenon has not so much been eliminated from modern life as shifted to different places. We have social practices in relation to which we are in a situation much like that of the Greeks with slavery. We recognise arbitrary and brutal ways in which people are handled by society, ways that are conditioned, often, by no more than exposure to luck. We have the intellectual resources to regard the situation of these people, and the systems that allow these things, as unjust, but are uncertain whether to do so, partly because we have seen the corruption and collapse of supposedly alternative systems, partly because we have no settled opinion on the question about which Aristotle tried to contrive a settled opinion, how far the existence of a worthwhile life for some people involves the imposition of suffering on others.[83]

This quotation underlines a fundamental problem with the language of rights. This language is radically egalitarian. Every human being is considered equal in terms of the rights that it possesses by mere virtue of being human. This language is also radically individualist: rights are fundamentally seen from the perspective of the individual. This seeming equality glosses over the fundamental fact that all modern societies are characterised by deep inequalities of power and wealth. And the combination of egalitarianism and individualism glosses over the existence of domination by one group over another in our societies.[84] In this respect, there are many reasons to think that the ancient perspective, which relies on a fundamental opposition between freedom and slavery/domination, can be immensely helpful in thinking about modern problems. In fact, in a recent influential book, the Australian political philosopher Philip Pettit has examined how the concept of freedom as non-domination can be used in order to re-order the fundamental institutions of our societies.[85] But much certainly still remains to be accomplished.

My second point concerns the deep fear of ancient freedom evident in the liberal mainstream of the last two centuries. In this view, fundamental rights have to be protected from the power of the state and, in particular, from the tyranny of a prejudiced majority. Widespread political participation is seen as a great danger to the preservation of rights and liberties given the hold of bigotry, ignorance and prejudice on wide sections of the population. Accordingly, it is necessary to put limits to popular sovereignty, and a bill of rights is the best way to effect this. There are, I think, two ways in which ancient history can challenge these claims. The first is the example of the Athenian democracy. We have seen that there was no theoretical limit to what the popular assembly, in which thousands of citizens participated, could decide. If the assembly wished to decide that all citizens should wear black clothes, there was nothing that could stop it from doing so. And yet, despite this potential totalitarian nightmare, Athens was considered the most tolerant society in ancient Greece. The opponents of democracy were particularly enraged by the lack of state supervision of private lives and what they considered as licence and insubordination. And the assembly largely abstained from instituting all these regulations of private life that we know existed in other Greek cities. Is this not verification of the idea that freedom can only be secured when there is widespread popular participation in the exercise of power? This was still well understood by the English liberal supporters of Athenian democracy in the nineteenth century, like John Stuart Mill:

> This remarkable testimony, as Mr. Grote has not failed to point out, wholly conflicts, so far as Athens is concerned, with what we are so often told about the entire sacrifice, in the ancient republics, of the liberty of the individual to an imaginary good of the state. In the greatest Greek commonwealth, as described by its most distinguished citizen, the public interest was held of paramount obligation in all things which concerned it; but, with that part of the conduct of individuals which concerned only themselves, public opinion did not interfere: while in the ethical practice of the moderns, this is exactly reversed, and no one is required by opinion to pay any regard to the

public, except by conducting his own private concerns in conformity to its expectations.[86]

Grote himself, the inventor of the modern image of Athenian democracy, was equally adamant that the link between political and individual freedom could only be retained through the performance of civic obligations.[87] Furthermore, it is an important lesson of the tradition that begins in plebeian Rome and reaches, through Machiavelli, the English opposition writers of the late seventeenth and eighteenth centuries that liberty has to be actively defended by constant vigilance. The mere enshrinement of liberty and rights in laws is inadequate and belies a passive understanding of liberty; on the contrary, it is the constant assertion of freedom in the public sphere that can guarantee the respect of even the most personal liberties.

The modern conception of liberty is also based, to an important extent, on the distinction between the private and the public sphere, or the civil society and the state. One of the main concerns of liberalism has been the protection of the private sphere and civil society from the encroachments of the state. In this respect, as we saw, the polemic against antiquity for failing to adhere to such a distinction played a fundamental role in the emergence of modern liberalism. Nevertheless, in the last few decades this distinction has been severely challenged. It is the greatest of ironies that this challenge came from feminism: women, of course, were completely excluded from the ancient conceptions of freedom. Many of the main demands of the feminist movement necessitate state intervention in the private sphere. Initially, the feminist movement considered that the abolition of discrimination in employment and pay would be sufficient to allow women equal opportunities to gain prosperity, success and security. But it soon became clear that there could not be any meaningful equal rights when, for example, job specifications were designed in such a way that they effectively barred women with children from being successful. Significant sections of the feminist movement have since called for state intervention within what is effectively the private sphere in order to enable women to achieve equality of rights.[88] It seems, therefore, that the separation between the public and the private and the location of liberty and individual rights in an inviolable private sphere is in need of radical rethinking.[89]

Finally, despite the attempt by liberal thinkers to denigrate the concept of freedom as self-mastery, which originated with Plato, I am not so certain that we can live without it. In fact, in real life, we normally take the denial of this concept as irrational. Certainly, anybody is free to kill himself by taking drugs or alcohol or by being obese, if one so wishes. And yet, we somehow also think that people who follow such paths are dominated by their lower selves and that as a community we should help such people to liberate themselves from their addictions. Why that principle, accepted by most people in this respect, should *prima facie* not apply to other facets of human life, is difficult to discern. In this respect, a dialogue with Plato and Rousseau still seems capable of generating important findings for the story of human freedom. The crucial distinction lies of course between helping and forcing people to liberate themselves from their lower selves. But we cannot deal with this dilemma until we consider different views concerning the end of man and the end of politics. This is the subject of our last chapter.

CHAPTER III

POLITICS AS ACTIVITY: PARTICIPATION, DELIBERATION, CONFLICT

This chapter will focus on politics seen as an activity. We have seen in the introduction that, as early as the archaic period, service to the community and thus participation in public affairs, deliberation and the regulation of conflict were seen as essential aspects of politics. We shall see how these activities were profoundly reconfigured due to the emergence of Athenian democracy and how ancient political practice and thought tried to deal with them.

Let us start with service to the community. Military service in defence of the community was the quintessential public service in the Homeric epics; and it remained so until citizenship and military service were finally dissociated under the Roman emperors. It is not difficult to see why military service remained the model par excellence of service to the community; the willingness to sacrifice one's life for the common good is the extreme example of the willingness to put the common good above anything else. In the archaic period we can see how service to the community became one of the most cherished activities in the Greek world. The transformation of Sparta during this period is the most eloquent example of a wider phenomenon.[1] The whole social fabric was refashioned in order to facilitate the needs of communal service. It is a process which is difficult for us to grasp, but which the ancient Greeks attributed unanimously to the legendary lawgiver Lycurgus. Young Spartans were taken away from their families at the age of eight, and undertook a vigorous public training in military practice, moral education and strict obedience, which to some extent lasted until their old age. The Spartans exercised no profession, since their needs were provided by the slave population of the helots; family life and privacy were significantly reconfigured, and Spartans passed most of their time in public, participating in public feasts, festivals and other activities and exercises.

Public service was an equally fundamental value in Athens, although it took a very different form there. The most influential tribute to the importance of public service and participation in Athens is the Funeral Oration that the historian Thucydides attributed to Pericles, the acclaimed leader of the Athenian democracy.[2]

> Our public men have, besides politics, their private affairs to attend to, and our ordinary citizens, though occupied with the pursuits of industry, are still fair judges of public matters; for, unlike any other nation, regarding him who takes no part in these duties not as unambitious but as useless, we are also the only ones who either make governmental decisions or at least frame the issues correctly.[3]

In contrast to the Spartans, most Athenians had to work to make a living; nevertheless, their devotion to public service was none the less significant, as Pericles testified. Athenian democracy was made possible by, but also facilitated, the mass participation of citizens in political activities and the performance of civic obligations.[4] This led to a reformulation of the language of service to the community and of *aretê*. *Aretê* was not anymore the personal excellence of the aristocratic hero; it now became the virtue that was required of citizens in order to perform their obligations and serve their community.[5] This transformation of *aretê* into civic virtue is best seen in the decrees of the Athenian democracy that bestowed honours on foreigners and citizens for services to the community. Honours were bestowed, because the said individual had shown himself '*agathos* to the Athenian people'; the old aristocratic term did not connote a social class any more, but it was appropriated to denote virtue towards the community.[6] As Pericles again phrased it in the Funeral Speech,

> But while the law secures equal justice to all alike in their private disputes, the claim of merit is also recognized; and when a citizen is in any way distinguished, he is preferred to the public service, not as a matter of privilege, but as the reward of *aretê*. Neither is poverty a bar, but a man may benefit his country whatever be the obscurity of his condition.[7]

Thus, Athenian democracy turned a value associated with a specific social class into a citizen trait that occupied a central place in Greek theoretical explorations of political activity.

But the emergence of democracy also affected the conception of deliberation as an essential feature of politics. Deliberation acquired a new role in Athenian politics. In contrast to most other cities, the executive power of Athenian magistrates was severely curtailed and they retained very little initiative of their own. All decisions of importance were taken by the citizen assembly. After the issue at hand was considered by the Council of the 500, the assembly was presented with the issue, or even with a specific proposal by the Council about how to deal with it; there followed an open debate, in which every citizen had the right to speak and the assembly had full power to accept, amend or turn down the motion of the Council and vote its own.[8] Thus, public mass deliberation became the most important political activity in Athens.

In tandem with this development, the nature of political leadership changed. Until the later fifth century, political leaders in Athens were recruited in the same way as in other non-democratic Greek polities. Political leaders usually belonged to a few families of birth and wealth, who were distinguished for their military exploits and based their power on a network of friends and relatives. The social and political elites were effectively identical. But, at that time, there emerged a new kind of political leaders.[9] These people were certainly rich, but they did not belong to the traditional aristocracy of birth and wealth; they based their power neither on their military exploits nor on a network of friends, but on their ability to persuade the mass assembly of the citizens to follow their advice and proposals. Thus, persuasive speech became the key element in Athenian politics.

It was these developments that put deliberation and rhetoric at the centre of Greek reflection on political activity. The problematic relationship between deliberation, knowledge and decision-making appeared as an issue at the very beginning of Greek political theory. An interesting comment appears in Herodotus' narration of the story of Aristagoras, the leader of the revolt of the Ionian cities against Persian rule. Aristagoras came to mainland Greece trying to enlist Sparta and Athens as allies. He failed to convince or to bribe the Spartan king Cleomenes in order to secure Spartan support. He then turned to the newly established Athenian democracy:

> Coming before the people, Aristagoras spoke to the same effect as at Sparta, of the good things of Asia, and how the Persians carried neither shield nor spear in war and could easily be overcome . . . There was nothing which he did not promise in the earnestness of his entreaty, till at last he prevailed upon them. It seems, then, that it is easier to deceive many than one, for he could not deceive Cleomenes of Lacedaemon, one single man, but thirty thousand Athenians he could.[10]

Athenian democracy had soon to face two important challenges to the role of mass deliberation in its functioning. How could an assembly with thousands of citizens, each of whom had the right to speak, ever come to any conclusion? And how could a state be governed, when every meeting of the assembly could, spurned by the passion of the moment, overturn the decisions of the previous meeting? Unscrupulous speakers would be able to mislead the people and make them adopt catastrophic policies; and a mass assembly would not be able to devise a stable policy. As long as power did not rest in some policy makers who would be able to guarantee stability and vision, successive assembly meetings could easily overturn previous policies and create chaos. In fact, in 411 BCE, these dangers came together, when a number of oligarchic politicians managed to convince the mass assembly to vote democracy out of existence!

Finally, the emergence of democracy had a lasting effect on Greek thought about political conflict. The earliest Greek reflections on conflict go back to the Homeric poems; and, even, in the archaic period, they identified conflict as a man-made phenomenon which could be dealt with by conscious human activity. The emergence of democracy expanded further the field of conflict. Political conflict was no longer restricted to elite politicians vying for power and honour. The opponents of political developments in Athens, who created the concept of democracy in order to castigate the new system as the rule of the poor, had discovered that the political field was invaded by social and economic groups vying for power to serve their own interests. Rich and poor, democrats and oligarchs, the elite and the mob, were new players in the political field who fought with each other mercilessly. But despite their insuperable differences, they all shared a common assumption. To understand what this assumption was, we need to pay attention to the vocabulary they used to describe and conceive it, because the choice of vocabulary had important implications. The Greek word for political conflict is *stasis*. *Stasis* originally meant 'to take a stand', 'to adopt a position', but it was used to describe all sorts of phenomena that we would describe in a different manner. It could mean a partisan political position, a faction, a party, conflict, political unrest, class struggle, civil war, revolution or the very disruption of the social fabric.[11] How could a single word describe all these very different phenomena? To understand this, we have to realise the background against which stasis is conceived. *Stasis* implied that an individual or a group adopted a particular position or engaged in activities that furthered their own personal or group interests, as opposed to furthering the common good. As the historian Moses Finley has put it,

The existence of classes and interests as an empirical fact [was], of course, not denied. What [was] denied is that the choice of political goals can legitimately be linked with these classes and interests, or that the good of the state can be advanced except by ignoring (if not suppressing) private interests.[12]

In other words, the existence of conflict was considered both inevitable and at the same time illegitimate. And the question of how a political community could avoid conflict became one of the constant preoccupations of Greek political thought.

These three aspect, participation, deliberation and conflict form the basis of Greek reflection on politics as an activity. Let us start our exploration by first looking at how Athenian democracy tried to deal with these three issues. To come to the issue of participation, despite the democratisation of virtue, the strong emphasis on the performance of services to the community was not without implications. In the passage quoted above, Pericles drew a distinction between the political leaders, who had enough leisure to dedicate themselves to politics and the formulation of policy, and the mass of ordinary citizens, who were obliged to spend most of their time working in order to make a living. Thus, those who possessed the wealth and leisure to devote themselves to public affairs enjoyed an elevation in their rank and status.[13] Athenian democracy tried to deal with the issue by instituting political pay for all citizens who devoted time to public service, whether as magistrates, assemblymen, jurymen, sailors, infantrymen or cavalrymen. But Athens was exceptional in the degree it decided to use communal resources to enhance the participation of the ordinary citizens. For most other political communities, from antiquity until modern times, the fact that the largest part of the population had to devote their time to making a living, provided a natural justification for confining the 'political nation' to an elite of leisure and wealth, which was able to devote itself to public affairs.

Athenian democracy responded in a number of different ways to the challenge of ensuring that mass deliberation worked. When democracy was restored in 403, after the brief oligarchic coup of the Thirty Tyrants, the Athenians devised a division of public decisions into laws and decrees. Laws were those public decisions which had general and permanent application, while decrees referred to specific circumstances. After the codification of those decisions which would be considered as laws, it was no longer possible for the assembly to vote new laws. The assembly from then onwards could only vote decrees, and no decree could contradict any of the laws already established. The modification of established laws and the introduction of new ones was thenceforth entrusted to a special body of lawgivers, which consisted of a thousand Athenian citizens selected by lot and convened every time there was a need for new legislation. Thus, the new rules made sure that the assembly could not be misled into disregarding the fundamental laws of the polity, while the selection of the lawgivers by lot would guarantee that legislative power would not be restricted to, or hijacked by, any specific group. The sovereignty of the laws became a fundamental element of Athenian political ideology.[14]

On the other hand, the Athenians came to generalise the procedure known as *graphê paranomôn*. This procedure entailed that a decision of the assembly could be challenged in a popular court for being contrary to the existing laws, or for being inexpedient. If the challenge was brought within a year from the passing of the decision, the proposer of the decision was personally liable, even if it had been unanimously accepted by the assembly, and, if found guilty, could be punished heavily. In this way, every speaker in the assembly became personally responsible for the advice he gave and would reap both the benefits and the penalties accruing from his proposals.[15]

Finally, how did Athens try to deal with the issue of conflict? The Athenians largely adopted an answer with traditional roots, but which also became one of the most important preoccupations of Greek political thought. In order to avoid conflict, it was necessary that citizens should put aside their own private and class interests and prioritise the pursuit of the common good. The answer to the problem of conflict was thus moral and educational. The citizens had to be educated into pursuing the common good.[16] The Athenians argued that many of their practices had, as an end, the education of the citizens in virtue. The civic discourse of their dramatic performances and festivals, the hortatory intention of their honorific inscriptions, the instruction and guidance of the laws were all seen as practices to educate citizens into pursuing the common good.

Let us now move on to see how Greek political thought grappled with the political questions brought into focus by Athenian democracy.[17] These experiences gave birth to a very fascinating work of political reflection: Thucydides' historical account of the Peloponnesian War between Athens and Sparta (431-404 BCE). Thucydides used the merciless struggle between the two great powers of his contemporary world to reflect on some fundamental problems of politics.[18] The Peloponnesian War provided the scene for internecine conflict between democrats and oligarchs, supporters of Athens and supporters of Sparta, rich and poor. Thucydides was the first author ever to present a large-scale historical narrative centred on political conflict and civil war.[19] His description of the development and escalation of political discord in the city of Corcyra has remained a classic of political thought ever since:

> *Stasis* ran its course from city to city, and the places it arrived at last, from having heard what had been done before carried to a still greater excess the refinement of their inventions . . . Words had to change their ordinary meaning and to take that which was now given them. Reckless audacity came to be considered the courage of a loyal ally; prudent hesitation, specious cowardice; moderation was held to be a cloak for unmanliness; ability to see all sides of a question, an inability to act on any. Frantic violence became the attribute of manliness; cautious plotting, a justifiable means of self-defence. The cause of all these evils was the lust for power arising from greed and ambition; and from these passions proceeded the violence of parties once engaged in contention. The leaders in the cities, each provided with the fairest professions . . . sought prizes for themselves in those public interests which they pretended to cherish, and, recoiling from no means in their struggles for ascendancy, engaged

in the direct excesses; in their acts of vengeance they went to even greater lengths, not stopping at what justice or the good of the state demanded.[20]

Thucydides explored in detail the role and forms of conflict in politics; but he also devoted a significant part of his work to reflections on the problem of political deliberation. His attention was caught by the new phenomenon of political leaders who based their power not on holding office, but on being able to convince the assembly to follow their policy. In his view, the Athenian defeat could be attributed to the inability of a mass assembly to devise a well-thought and consistent policy, the dangers of irresponsible political rhetoric, and the failure of political leadership. Thucydides depicted two starkly contrasting models of political leadership and rhetoric. His positive model was exemplified by Pericles, who was presented as a leader who was able to conceive what was best for the community and convince his citizens to follow it. The rhetoric of Pericles was able to tame the wild beast of the mass assembly and educate the citizens through argument and exhortation. On the opposite side were the demagogues, who, because they lacked the stature of a statesman like Pericles, were keen to follow and fulfil the wildest desires and wishes of the people, instead of resisting them and showing them what was truly good.[21] Since Thucydides, demagogy became a chief concern of political philosophy.

The problems of political activity as exemplified by Athenian democracy also formed the background for the political thought of the fourth-century philosopher Plato. Plato questioned the way Athenians practiced mass deliberation:

Now I observe that when we meet together in the assembly, and the matter in hand relates to building, the builders are summoned as advisers; when the question is one of shipbuilding, then the shipwrights; and the like of other arts which they think capable of being taught and learned. And if some person offers to give them advice who is not supposed by them to have any skill in the art, even though he be good-looking, and rich, and noble, they will not listen to him, but laugh and hoot at him, until . . . he is clamoured down and retires of himself. This is their way of behaving about professors of the arts. But when the question is an affair of state, then everybody is free to have a say–carpenter, tinker, cobbler, sailor, passenger; rich and poor, high and low–anyone who likes gets up, and no-one reproaches him, as in the former case, with not having learned, and having no teacher, and yet giving advice.[22]

In this passage Plato raised, for the first time in political theory, the issue of politics as a form of knowledge. Politics is like any other activity which needs to apply a specific set of expertise in order to achieve a certain aim. By giving the ability to speak to any citizen, irrespective of whether he had the relevant expertise or not, the Athenians were jeopardising their prospects for success. But his disagreement with Athenian-style deliberation went even deeper. The very form of assembly deliberation made it impossible for Athenians to arrive at the correct answers to their problems, because it was dominated by unscrupulous orators who were only pandering to the prejudices and wishes of the masses. Majority voting was absurd, because, no matter how many people voted against a proposal, this could never be an argument against its truthfulness. Plato used the philosophical dialogue in his works to show that only the dialectical exchange of arguments between speakers could enable them to change their views and arrive at the truth. Demagogic oratory coupled with majority voting was no means towards this end.

This conception of politics as knowledge provided Plato with an answer to the problems of deliberation and conflict. Viewing political activity as a field of applying expertise and experience dispensed with both deliberation and conflict. The doctor does not need to deliberate with his patients about their medical treatment; he knows the answer to the problem, while the patients do not. And conflict is irrelevant, because the patients must accept that the doctor knows what is in their best interests, even though they might not like it. Of course, one has to ensure that the doctor does act in the patient's best interest; but this is again a problem of the moral education of the political actor. If politics is an activity that requires sufficient knowledge to be performed successfully, it follows that participation in deliberation and the authority to take decisions should be restricted to those who possess this necessary knowledge.[23]

Aristotle, Plato's former student, was the first to write a systematic account of politics in his famous *Politics*.[24] Aristotle's approach to politics as an activity seems to waver between different and often contrasting tendencies. This is one reason that Aristotle's political thought has been so influential: thinkers with very different views and approaches can rely on different aspects of his thought or emphasise different issues. In one way Aristotle can be read as the quintessential partisan of the value and the necessity of politics as an activity. He famously described man as a political animal and gave an explanation of why this was so:

> And why man is a political animal in a greater measure than any bee or any gregarious animal is clear. For nature, as we declare, does nothing without purpose; and man alone of the animals possesses speech. The mere voice, it is true, can indicate pain and pleasure, and therefore is possessed by the other animals as well (for their nature has been developed so far as to have sensations of what is painful and pleasant and to indicate those sensations to one another), but speech is designed to indicate the advantageous and the harmful, and therefore also the right and the wrong; for it is the special property of man in distinction from the other animals that he alone has perception of good and bad and right and wrong and the other moral qualities, and it is partnership in these things that makes a household and a polis.[25]

The ability to distinguish between right and wrong, which is expressed through rational speech, is what makes human beings particularly fit to live in a political community. Thus speech and reason, which in Greek are expressed by the very same word *logos*, are fundamental aspects of being human and define the activity of politics.

Furthermore, Aristotle placed great importance on the value of political participation. His definition of citizenship as 'taking part in deliberative or judicial office' put the emphasis on the active exercise of political capacities.[26] One of the most memorable aspects of his ideal state is the praise of 'political' rule, in which citizens take turns in ruling and being ruled.[27] Aristotle clearly conceived the political community as a field in which one can achieve virtue and nobility. By participating in politics, by ruling and being ruled, the citizen practiced prudence and became virtuous. This is the reason that Aristotle's ideal state had as one of its main functions how to educate its citizens in virtue. But his emphasis on virtue as the defining feature of a political association led him to the paradoxical conclusion that if in a community a certain individual is paramount in virtue, he should rule as a monarch, and 'political rule' by turns in office would be redundant. Although Aristotle clearly thought that this circumstance would be quite uncommon, it is nevertheless doubtless that he agreed that a polity without political activity could indeed be ideal.[28]

Even more, Aristotle was reluctant to identify the good man and the good citizen. Although in his ideal polity they would be identical (by excluding the vast majority of inhabitants from being citizens), in most actual polities the virtuous individual will not be identical with the virtuous citizen. Finally, although the virtuous man would and should participate in political activities and assume office if it was possible, Aristotle never claimed that such participation is essential for a virtuous human being. Many activities, which according to Aristotle allowed men to exercise virtue, were not political in the stricter sense: activities like participating in a friendship or a religious group. Aristotle called these activities political because they were part of the life of the polis and they constituted associations which were subsumed by the wider political community. Thus, Aristotle's attitude towards politics was ambiguous: although he could look at it in a positive light, he never deemed it as an essential part of being human and virtuous.[29]

Furthermore, Aristotle was very much aware that conflict is an ineradicable part of politics.[30] In fact, a large part of the *Politics* is devoted to an in-depth study of *stasis*. More than any other ancient political thinker, Aristotle analysed the various reasons and motives that generated political conflict. These reasons ranged from disagreement over rival definitions of justice and equality to the pursuit of honour, power and self-interest by groups and individuals. His methodical analysis of the causes and directions of political conflict provided later thinkers with a rich repertoire of cases and solutions. While Aristotle claimed that political participation is ennobling, at the same time it is clear that, given the constituent features of most citizens, widespread political participation could only lead to a further escalation of *stasis* and conflict. Thus, one of the most striking features of the *Politics* is Aristotle's seeking of various different ways in which conflict could be minimised; and when the implication seemed clear that this could be effected only through curtailing political activities he seemed to have no second thoughts in suggesting this course.

Aristotle made the pursuit of stability one of the paramount criteria of a successful polity. Since democrats and oligarchs, rich and poor, the elite and the mass could not be expected to pursue the common good and avoid factional conflict, Aristotle tried to find ways in which these conflicts could be contained and mitigated. His preferred solution would be an extensive middle class that would stand as a buffer between the rich and the poor and bring stability and moderation to political life.[31] But he realistically recognised that few communities ever exhibited this middle class. A different solution posited that a balance could be found through the mixing of the opposite political principles of democracy and aristocracy. The democrats would be appeased by adopting the principle of universal suffrage for all citizens, while the aristocrats would be satisfied by the principle of restricting election into office to only a section of the citizens.[32] Finally, Aristotle argued that the problems created by deliberation in an assembly, which is able to decide on any course of action and often ends up with the poor majority subjugating the rich minority, could be dealt with through a strict adherence to the rule of law: he supported the adoption of a number of fundamental laws which could not be flouted by the decisions of the assembly.[33]

Aristotle's view that, in certain conditions, the rule of law is preferable to the rule of men would have a great future.

We should finish our exploration of Greek views with an important Hellenistic contribution. This contribution was based on a pragmatic description of Roman politics by Polybius. According to Polybius, Rome had a mixed constitution, as we have seen. But in contrast to Sparta, whose mixed constitution was created by Lycurgus, the legendary lawgiver, the Roman constitution was the piecemeal product of historical evolution and accommodation. The stability of the Roman constitution was mainly based on fear. It depended on the fact that none of the three elements could exercise power on its own. The fear of the other elements meant that each element kept its proper place and did not try to overwhelm the others. This stability, created by a balance of fear, meant that Rome was able to avoid the constitutional cycle that every political community was destined to pass through. The inherent contradictions of every simple constitution that led to its collapse and transformation were halted in Rome by being balanced by the other elements. Polybius did not believe that the process of transformation could be halted for ever; neither did he base his presentation of Rome on any normative ideas about the proper distribution of power.[34] He merely described what he thought of as the successful result of a historical process. Nevertheless, his vision of Rome as a solution to the problem of stability and success was destined to have a glorious afterlife, as we shall see.

The Roman attitude to politics as an activity was less ambivalent than that of the Greeks. Service to the community and political participation were seen as the paramount activities of a worthy life. For the Romans, the establishment of one's *virtus* and the pursuit of *gloria* were the supreme aims for every man; but these aims could only be achieved by serving the community, holding office and performing great deeds in counsel and war. The pursuit of political office was the only honourable course open to the man who had the qualifications (ancestry, wealth, leisure, talent).[35] It is impressive that, even when Roman authors defended their abstention from active participation and the pursuit of other activities (e.g. writing philosophy or history) as forced on them by the circumstances, they still felt the need to argue that these other activities were merely a different way of serving the community by other means; it is characteristic that neither Aristotle nor Plato felt the same need to justify the pursuit of the contemplative life.[36] This dedication to the political life was formalised to the extent that the Romans developed the *cursus honorum*: a sequential ordering of public offices that aspiring citizens had to follow. The epitaphs of Roman statesmen advertised in the first place the various political offices they had held during their lives.

What was the Roman contribution to this reflection on the nature and problems of the political activity? In order to assess this contribution, we have to bear in mind that all texts that have survived come either from the last few decades of the Roman republic, when the Roman system of political activity had broken down, or from the imperial period, when the character of politics had fundamentally changed. It is the works of Cicero, the Roman politician and philosopher, which represent the most profound Roman discussion of politics that has survived. His work *On Duties* expressed for generations of modern thinkers from the Renaissance onwards the quintessence of the Roman view of politics and the role of the political actor.[37] A famous orator himself, Cicero presented in a variety of works the importance of political oratory and deliberation for the proper function of the political community.[38] Finally, he defended the *vita activa* of participation in politics and service to the community as the supreme end of human life:

> I make this one assertion: nature has given men such a need for virtue and such a desire to defend the common safety that this force has overcome all the enticements of pleasure and ease. Furthermore, virtue is not some kind of knowledge to be possessed without using it: even if the intellectual possession of knowledge can be maintained without use, virtue consists entirely in its employment; moreover, its most important employment is the governance of states and

the accomplishment in deeds rather than words of the things that philosophers talk about in their corners.[39]

Where Aristotle had presented an ambivalent evaluation of the political activity, Cicero provided a wholehearted expression of praise.

But it was during the rule of the emperors that a number of texts, which would later play an extremely influential role in modern attempts to deal with the problem of politics, came to light. This is by no means a coincidence. In the changed political environment of the empire, where the effective locus of power had shifted to a court, the glorious past had an exceedingly important role to play. The works of Livy, Plutarch, Seneca and Tacitus presented later readers with highly influential accounts of ancient politics.

Livy was a Roman historian who lived at the time of Augustus. His *History* covered the entire period from the foundation of Rome to his own time in painstaking detail. Livy memorably depicted the acts of the virtuous heroes who had given their lives for their country, saved her from ruin and managed to extend her power to the borders of the then known world. Due to accidents of preservation, the text that survived in modern times mainly covered the early years of Rome and the middle republic, while the parts covering the period of civil war and crisis from the time of the Gracchi were largely lost. Thus, Livy's work came fundamentally to be seen as a repository of Roman virtue.[40] If Cicero had defended theoretically the importance of public service to the community as a supreme value, Livy presented a vast canvas of Romans who had followed that path with utmost self-denial. Plutarch was a Greek author who lived in the first century CE under the Roman Empire. His most important work in this context, the *Parallel Lives of Illustrious Greeks and Romans*, brought together Greek and Roman virtue by presenting memorable portraits of ancient politicians and generals: Greeks like Aristides, Phocion and Pelopidas and Romans like Brutus, Cato the Elder and Cato the Younger.[41] It was in these works that modern Europeans would later encounter models of citizens and statesmen who had devoted their lives in pursuing the common good and serving their community.

If Livy and Plutarch presented the long gone world of the virtuous heroes, Seneca, a philosopher and tutor of Nero, kept his attention to the problems of his contemporary world and attempted to provide a normative account of what politics under a monarch should be like.[42] The virtues of the citizen and statesman that Greek and Roman political thought had long explored were now transferred to the figure of the monarch. If the ruler managed to exhibit and practice these virtues, then justice, safety, stability and prosperity would be guaranteed for his subjects. With Seneca, the important political question became the education of the monarch into the virtues necessary for ruling the state.

Finally, in contrast to Seneca, Cornelius Tacitus presented the realistic side of court politics and introduced a very different conception of political activity.[43] Tacitus, a contemporary of Plutarch, wrote the *Annals* and the *Histories*, two historical works narrating Roman history in the first century CE and in particular the civil war of CE 69. The old politics of participation, public service and deliberation was by then long gone; Tacitus described a world in which virtue was eclipsed and corruption and tyranny reigned supreme. The senate, the old centre of wise and virtuous politicians, had become a supine organ of the emperors and only a few heroic individuals dared dissent, thus forfeiting their lives. But Tacitus presented in detail a new form of politics that was centred on a ruler and his efforts to maintain his power and stifle opposition and conflict through various techniques of dissimulation and suppression. It is notoriously difficult to ascertain what were Tacitus's own personal views;[44] the speeches he inserted in his historical narrative could give voice to very different views and could be interpreted in very different ways. It was thus a work which could lend itself to very different interpretations.

We can now summarise the various ancient understandings of politics as an activity and its attendant problems. Politics could be seen as a service to the community and a dedication to the common good; we have seen how in Athens, Sparta and Rome there emerged various discourses that sought to praise active participation in public life and achieving glory through serving the community. On the other hand, politics was also connected to deliberation and conflict; from the fifth century BCE onwards the relationship between participation, deliberation and conflict became a primary focus of political thought. One influential answer among ancient thinkers was the emphasis on virtue. If those who participated in politics were virtuous, they would be incorruptible and able to put the common interest above their personal or class interest; they would be able to deliberate and advise in the best manner, instead of demagogically deceiving the people; conflict would be avoided or minimised, since the citizens would be able to pursue the common good. The education of citizens in virtue was thus the key problem for a polity and corruption the key danger.

A second answer, while not discounting the first one, put little faith in virtue as the sole means of solving political problems and attempted to find a solution by institutional means. Aristotle saw in the rule of law or the preponderance of the middle classes the possibility of overcoming class interests and achieving political stability, while Polybius presented Rome as a polity in which the consuls, the senate and the people achieved greatness through a stability of fear and interest. Finally, Plato provided an answer to the political problem by eliminating politics completely. In his approach politics was identified with a form of knowledge; accordingly, those who possessed the knowledge necessary to steer the ship of state should be given the power to exercise this form of knowledge. Deliberation was unnecessary and conflict could thus be eliminated.

The moderns

The political thought of antiquity survived through the Middle Ages mainly through the genre of the 'Mirror of Princes', works which aimed to educate princes and rulers into the tasks of ruling. The main focus of these works was an examination of the virtues that were necessary for a ruler in order to exercise properly his function. In this respect, the ancient works on virtue and power and the ancient equivalents to the Mirrors were of profound importance.[45] But, in the course of the fourteenth and fifteenth centuries, a new discourse of politics emerged in Italy.[46] The city-states of the Italian peninsula were governed in a very different manner from of that of feudal principalities or kingdoms. In their struggle against kingdoms and city-states dominated by *signori*, those city-states that were still governed as a community of citizens, primarily Florence and Venice, rediscovered and appropriated an ancient discourse of talking about politics. Petrarch, one of the first humanists, was aghast in discovering that Cicero in his old age had abandoned his philosophical writings and returned to active politics, and castigated him for betraying the contemplative life; but later humanists would use Cicero as a model for every citizen to follow. Aristotle's *Politics* and Cicero's *On Duties* were instrumental in creating a language of politics that stressed the supreme value of the *vita activa* and participation in public affairs.[47] In contrast to other political languages, which presented people as subjects of a ruler, civic humanism, as modern historians have called this language, put the focus on the citizen and his participation in politics. Adopting the Ciceronian position, it identified the good man with the good citizen who takes active part in politics by serving his community through deeds and words, thus achieving fame and glory. The good citizen must be virtuous, for he has to put the public good above his own personal interest. After its initial emergence in Italy, this language was exported to the rest of Europe and became a very significant means of thinking about politics in various national traditions.[48]

Machiavelli inherited to an important extent this tradition of civic humanism; but at the same time he initiated a revolution in thinking about politics.[49] Virtue remained an essential concept in his political thought; but he departed from classical political and ethical thought in completely dissociating virtue from justice and morality. Virtue for him was 'a willingness to do whatever may be necessary for the attainment of civic glory and greatness, whether the actions involved happen to be intrinsically good or evil in character'.[50] Machiavelli doubted that the human capacity for rational speech allowed humans to move from a calculation of their own personal interest to an understanding of what is just and good for everybody. Thus, he went against the mainstream of ancient political thought in this respect.[51]

> All writers on politics have pointed out, and throughout history there are plenty of examples which indicate, that in constituting and legislating for a commonwealth it must be taken for granted that all men are wicked and that they will always give vent to the malignity that is in their minds when opportunity offers.[52]

Given such a view of human nature, corruption, defined as the tendency to put personal interest above the common good and civic glory, was a constant threat for all human polities. The most innovative part of Machiavelli's work was the insight that a polity could use institutional means to force citizens to uphold the common good despite their selfish nature, or indeed because of it. The answer was an institutionalisation of conflict and fear.

Machiavelli relied precisely on antiquity to furnish him with an image of this alternative solution. Polybius's interpretation of the Roman republic provided him with an historical illustration of his principles. We have already seen how he distinguished two *humori*, the patricians and the plebeians. Machiavelli believed that the propensity of the elite to acquire honour and power was so strong, that any polity that did not grant them enough honour, and opportunities to acquire it, was bound to be destabilised or overthrown. On the other hand, this propensity was deeply dangerous for the stability of the polity; therefore it was necessary to curb it. In Machiavelli's view it was the people that were best placed to play this role, since they only wished not to be dominated and to be left alone to pursue their tasks. The people could play this role if there existed institutional opportunities to express their anger and chastise the elite, like the impeachment of politicians in Rome. Through these institutional means, the elite would be kept in place and forced to pursue the common good:

The institutions which caused the Roman republic to return to its start were the introduction of the plebeian tribunes, censorship and all the other laws which put a check on human ambition and arrogance; to which institutions life must be given by some virtuous citizen who cooperates strenuously in giving them effect despite the power of those who contravene them.[53]

Machiavelli through his reading of Roman politics and history opened the path for the acceptance of conflict as an essential and even beneficial aspect of politics and the defence of interest as a legitimate political aim. Machiavelli's negation of virtue in its classical sense as an essential element of politics was also important because it made possible the inclusion of every citizen in the political process. We have seen how a politics of virtue had overtly elitist tones, since the majority of citizens did not have the education and the leisure necessary to devote themselves to public affairs. But, once the defence of property and interest becomes an essential aspect of politics, even the poorest citizen can be seen as a political actor in attempting to protect his own interests.[54]

Machiavelli's discarding of justice as part of virtue was best seen in his famous *Prince*, which was a manual of advice to rulers on how to secure their rule and enhance their power.[55] Machiavelli had presented it to the Medici, the new rulers of Florence after the demise of the republic in 1512. This overthrow was characteristic of a larger tendency all over Europe: the growing control of resources by rulers and monarchs and their increasing efforts to increase their power. These rulers were interested in a very different form of political activity, and they needed practical advice on how to achieve their aims. Machiavelli had tried to fill the gap, but *The Prince* was widely condemned as immoral and irreligious. One solution for those still willing to provide advice was to turn to the ancient texts once more. They could reinterpret the works of Cicero, or at least emphasise different aspects from those which had commanded attention until then. Thus, Cicero's statement that 'the safety of the people is the supreme law' and his discussion of the issue could be used in order to justify a ruler's adoption of extreme measures in order to secure the peace and safety of his subjects.[56]

But it was mainly through recourse to Tacitus, an author who had been largely forgotten until then, that a new conception of politics was debated and formed. Between 1580 and 1700 more than a hundred writers wrote commentaries on Tacitus, ranging from thinly disguised political treatises on modern concerns to serious commentaries, which aimed to discover the political wisdom of Tacitus and its relevance to the modern world.[57] Given the notorious difficulty of establishing Tacitus's own views, it is hardly surprising that his authority could be used to support the most diverse arguments. Modern scholars have distinguished between the 'red' Tacitists, those who used Tacitus in order to decry arbitrary rule and the new form of politics, and the 'black' Tacitists, those who used Tacitus to support reason of state policies. All these authors, nevertheless, shared a similar technique. They would extract opinions and aphorisms from Tacitus's text and use them in order to construct a systematic approach to the problems facing early modern absolutist states in recurrent conditions of civil war. Tacitus was thus instrumental in constructing a political discourse, the focus of which was not political participation, deliberation and public service, but the maintenance of stability and the protection of the interests of the ruler and the state.

Other authors chose to dissociate politics from participation, conflict and deliberation through a head-on attack on ancient authorities. The most influential of these authors was Hobbes. It is interesting to note, however that Hobbes used the ancient authors in order to formulate his thinking, to illustrate his thoughts, but also to decry what was dangerous about ancient political thought and its imitation. Hobbes had a thorough humanist education, as was natural in his time; it is, therefore, not surprising that his first important published work was a famous translation of Thucydides' history of the Peloponnesian War, together with an important introduction.[58] Thucydides exerted a formative influence on Hobbes's thought.[59] Thucydides' narrative provided Hobbes with the raw material for his state of nature, with its brutal and constant warfare of each against each.[60] But Thucydides could also be used in order to make sense of the traumatic experience of the English Civil War;[61] his description of the civil war in Corcyra was a potent image of what could happen when civil authority broke down and conflict reached its limits. Thucydides' analysis of the process that led to political conflict was an excellent reminder of the necessity to provide a means of avoiding such a potential of political activity. But Thucydides was also important in showing the potential dangers of political deliberation, as Hobbes commented:

> In those days it was impossible for any man to give good and profitable counsel for the commonwealth and not incur the displeasure of the people. For their opinion was such of their own power, and of the facility of achieving whatsoever action they undertook, that such men only swayed the assemblies, and were esteemed wise and good commonwealth's men, as did put them upon the most dangerous and desperate enterprises. Whereas he that gave them temperate and discreet advice, was thought a coward, or not to understand, or else to malign their power. . .And it holdeth much more in a multitude, than in one man. For a man that reasoneth with himself, will not be ashamed to admit of timorous suggestions in his business, that he may the stronglier provide; but in public deliberations before a multitude, fear (which for the most part adviseth well, though it execute not so) seldom or never sheweth itself or is admitted. By this means it came to pass amongst the Athenians, who thought they were able to do anything, that wicked men and flatterers drove them headlong into those actions that were to ruin them; and the good men either durst not oppose, or if they did, undid themselves.[62]

Hobbes's solution avoided the pitfalls of both conflict and demagogic rhetoric by entrusting all authority to a single locus of power, which he called sovereign. This sovereign was seen as an artificial entity which guaranteed the peace and security of every member of the community. The modern conception of the political community as the abstract and neutral form of the state and the identification of politics with the interests of the state rather than with public service and citizen deliberation is, to an important extent, attributable to Hobbes.[63]

Hobbes's solution was strongly challenged by the other major thinker of the English Revolution: James Harrington. Harrington's thought is another interesting example of the mixture of ancient influences and modern rejections of key premises of ancient thought.[64] Like Machiavelli and Hobbes, Harrington was unwilling to believe that rational speech could create an understanding of the common good or that virtue could guarantee its pursuit. In contrast to Machiavelli, he was not willing to accept tumults and faction as the price of political success.

> There is not a more noble or useful question in the politics than that which is started by Machiavel: whether means were to be found whereby the enmity that was between the senate and the people of Rome might have been removed.[65]

Unlike Hobbes, he was not willing to accept the elimination of politics as a welcome answer to the vagaries of political conflict. His solution was to create an institutional machine that would guarantee political stability and success without presupposing virtuous citizens. This was, of course, a primarily modern solution; but it was the political experience and institutional practice of the ancient polities, what he called 'ancient prudence', that furnished him with the elements of his system. Harrington defined ancient prudence in the following way:

> Relation being had to these two times, government (to define it *de jure*, or according to antient prudence) is an art whereby a civil society of men is instituted and preserv'd upon the foundation of common right or interest; or (to follow Aristotle and Livy) it is the empire of laws, and not of men.[66]

Harrington wanted to create a popular government but without political participation and its dangers. His solution was greatly influenced by Sparta. He believed that the proper function of a polity depended on a natural aristocracy; this was no longer an aristocracy of descent, title or wealth, but an aristocracy of talent and wisdom. Sparta was the ideal example; for, as he pointed out, Sparta, in contrast to Rome and her division between patricians and plebeians, had no aristocracy proper, but an elite of wise men selected by the community as a whole.[67] This natural aristocracy would make possible the proper function of a system in which every member of the community would have a say. The ignorance and stupidity of the rest of the citizens made it dangerous to entrust them with important political decisions; unscrupulous demagogues could easily point them in the wrong direction with their rhetoric.[68] A stable and successful political system should find a way to recruit the natural aristocracy as its governing elite; but how could one guarantee that the natural aristocracy would not abuse its position, given Harrington's unwillingness to base his system on mere virtue?

This would be achieved by means of a distinction between two bodies: a deliberative council consisting of the natural aristocracy of the commonwealth, which would debate and propose legislative measures, and a council consisting of representatives of the whole community, which would not be allowed to deliberate or propose, but only to vote on the proposed measures.[69] He illustrated his proposal with a famous simile of two girls dividing a piece of cake: one girl would make the division and the other one would choose which piece to take.[70] Deliberation was the proper activity for the natural aristocracy; but, if one entrusted them also with decision-making, they could abuse their position to further only their own group interests. Therefore, the solution was to restrict decision-making to the rest of the citizens. Since the natural aristocracy would know that its proposals could only be made into law if they were accepted by the rest of the citizens, they would have to propose measures that took account of the common good, and not only their personal interests, if legislation was to pass. On the other hand, the decision-making assembly was strictly forbidden from discussing or amending the proposed measures; this could only lead to demagoguery and faction. Instead, they could only accept or reject the proposed meas-ures, thus ensuring that they would accept those measures that promoted the common good, while rejecting those measures which did not. The Spartan *Gerousia*, made up of the natural aristocracy of the community, which had the right to debate and propose, and the Spartan Apella, which had the right only to vote on the proposals, offered the best model of emulation in Harrington's view.[71] Sparta provided the example of a meritocratic governing elite not based on privilege and wealth, an example which would prove of great influence in the future. Most importantly the representative system would allow every citizen to have a say of some sorts, while avoiding popular participation and agitation.

As with his contribution to the classification of regimes, Montesquieu had a very influential role in the reformulation of this discussion during the eighteenth century.[72] There is little doubt that Montesquieu deeply admired the numerous examples of self-sacrifice for the community and virtuous service of the common good that he could find in Livy and Plutarch:

> The political men of Greece who lived under popular government recognised no other force to sustain it than virtue. Those of today speak to us only of manufacturing, commerce, finance, wealth and even luxury.[73]

> Most of the ancient peoples lived in governments that had virtue for their principle, and, when that virtue was in full force, things were done in those governments that we no longer see and that astonish our small souls.[74]

But, at the same time, he was deeply convinced that virtue was no longer an option in the modern commercial and deeply inegalitarian societies of Europe. What could be the answer in modern circumstances? Montesquieu had effectively two different answers. One was that modern political systems were based on different principles form those of the ancient republics and could be successful even without virtue. While republics were based on virtue, monarchies were based on honour and despotisms on fear. The second answer was destined to exert even greater influence. He argued that virtue could be redundant in the political process, if there was a division of power between executive, legislative and judicial branches. This division of power, which Montesquieu saw enshrined in the British constitution, would ensure that no single branch would be able to abuse its power without being checked by the other two. The distinction and balance between the monarchical, aristocratic and democratic elements of the mixed constitution that Polybius had described, were transformed by Montesquieu into a distinction between three branches of government, that would keep each other in place through fear and interdependence.

The search for a solution to the problems of politics that did not depend on virtue became particularly pronounced in eighteenth-century Britain. The thinkers of the Scottish Enlightenment further amplified the discoveries of Montesquieu by insisting on the fundamental differences between ancient and modern politics. Adam Ferguson was one of the most influential representatives of this group of thinkers.[75] Ferguson was adamant that modern polities differed from ancient ones in the means they used in order to maintain peace and stability:

> Where men enjoy peace, they owe it either to their mutual regards and affections, or to the restraints of law. Those are the happiest states which procure peace to their members by the first of these methods: But it is sufficiently uncommon to procure it even by the second. The first would withhold the occasions of war and of competition. The second adjusts the pretensions of men by stipulations and treaties. Sparta taught her citizens not to regard interest: Other free nations secure the interest of their members, and consider this as a principal part of their rights.[76]

For Ferguson ancient politics were dominated by violence and demagoguery; these problems could be solved by entrusting political decisions to a body of representatives. In his work on the history of the Roman republic, Ferguson put his case in characteristic terms:

> Great part of the [harm] might have been prevented, if the plebeians, now in possession of the right to nominate tribunes for the care of their interests, had from thenceforward been content with the power of election merely, had discontinued their own collective assemblies for any other purpose, and encreased the number of tribunes to a just representative of their whole body. The return, however, was more agreeable to the spirit of times. The people were allowed to assemble; and, instead of a representation to support and preserve their rights with steadiness and with moderation, they proceeded to elect a few leaders, who, from thenceforward, were to head every popular tumult and to raise up every wind of contention into a storm.[77]

These ideas became paramount in the debates that followed the American Revolution and the establishment of a new state on the other side of the Atlantic. The spectre of ancient politics was constantly before the statesmen and legislators who were faced with the unparalleled opportunity to create a new political system from scratch. On the one hand, the heroes of Livy and Plutarch, with their paramount virtue and self-negating dedication to the common good were greatly admired and seen as models of what America would need in the aftermath of its overthrowing the British yoke. But, after victory in the War of Independence, the bitter experiences of faction and corruption and the threat of events like Shay's Rebellion forced some American politicians and intellectuals to think anew the kind of politics they were aiming at. We have already encountered the *Federalist Papers*, the most original of the works that emanated from this crisis. The authors of the *Federalist Papers* were constantly haunted by the fear that American politics would come to resemble the worst excesses of the ancient republics.

It is impossible to read the history of the petty republics of Greece and Italy, without feeling sensations of horror and disgust at the distractions with which they were continually agitated, and at the rapid succession of revolutions, by which they were kept perpetually vibrating between the extremes of tyranny and anarchy.[78]

They were equally concerned about the dangers of allowing the people to participate in deliberation:

In all very numerous assemblies of whatever characters composed, passion never fails to wrest the sceptre from reason. Had every Athenian citizen been a Socrates, every Athenian assembly would still have been a mob.[79]

We have already seen how they advocated representation and election as a means to avoid the dangers inherent in direct popular participation in deliberation and government. But it is equally interesting to note how they provided a solution that could dispense with virtue as the necessary element in avoiding conflict and fostering the common good. Self-interest could instead be counted upon to provide the foundation on which a stable political system could be built. But what was there to guarantee that the pursuit of self-interest would not further accelerate conflict and faction? The answer was that faction could not be eliminated, as it was part of human nature; but it could be regulated and made into a positive element of the system. The problem was that faction in the ancient republics was particularly internecine, because of their small size: it was easy in such a setting for the whole citizen body to be divided in two rival factions. But in a modern large republic this problem could be sidestepped:

The other point of difference is, the greater number of citizens, and extent of territory, which may be brought within the compass of republican, than of democratic government; and it is this circumstance principally which renders factious combinations less to be dreaded in the former, than in the latter. The smaller the society, the fewer probably will be the distinct parties and interests composing it; the fewer the distinct parties and interests, the more frequently will a majority be found of the same party; and the smaller the number of individuals composing a majority, and the smaller the compass within which they are placed, the more easily will they concert and execute their plans of oppression.[80]

Thus, the Federalists, in their effort to avoid the pitfalls of ancient politics, had finally come up with the conception of politics and political activity we are still familiar with. Representation was the means to achieve legitimacy without the dangers of demagoguery and extensive citizen participation; the pursuit of self-interest was a legitimate means of achieving political aims and of keeping the balance between different individuals and groups; and political parties were not an evil of faction, but a means of legitimately pursuing self-interest.[81]

Montesquieu's depiction of virtue as the characteristic feature of ancient politics proved a great inspiration for thinkers who were otherwise reluctant to accept his further premise that ancient politics were irrelevant in a modern context. It was again Rousseau who proved the most influential of these thinkers. From his earliest works he repudiated the pursuit of interest as a legitimate political activity and espoused virtue and the pursuit of the common good. Already in his *Discourse on the Arts and Sciences* (1751) Sparta and Rome were presented as model political communities in which citizens were virtuous and willing to sacrifice themselves for the defence of their country and the common good. They stood as mirrors to Rousseau's contemporary polities, where corruption had all but eclipsed virtue. The pursuit of self-interest could only drive communities apart; it promoted strife and inequality, and thus dissociated the citizens from their community and its institutions. Only if the citizens learned to love their community and support its institutions could a community and its members flourish. How could this be achieved? Like Montesquieu, Rousseau stressed that social and economic equality and frugality were necessary for creating civic virtue and attachment to the country; the citizen who was destitute and propertiless had no motive to defend his community; the citizen who lived in luxury had no inkling to sacrifice his convenience for the service of the community. But Rousseau went further than Montesquieu in stressing the value of civic participation for creating this feeling of attachment and patriotism. Rousseau thus widened the notion of political participation: participation in the assembly was part of a wider genus of civic activities that aimed to create solidarity among the citizens and love of country and its institutions. It is obvious that the ancient republics provided Rousseau with the ideal model of his political community:

> It was the same spirit that guided all the ancient legislators in their work of creating institutions. They all sought bonds that might attach citizens to the fatherland and to one another; and they found them in peculiar usages, in religious ceremonies, which, by their very nature, were always national and exclusive; in games which kept citizens frequently assembled; in exercises which increased not only their vigour and strength but also their pride and self-esteem; in spectacles which, by reminding them of the history of their ancestors, their misfortunes, their virtues, their victories, touched their hearts, inflamed them with a lively spirit of emulation and attached them strongly to that fatherland with which they were meant to be incessantly preoccupied.[82]

But what about politics in the stricter sense of the term? We have seen how Rousseau posited an assembly of all citizens as the only means of expressing the general will. How did Rousseau face the problems of deliberation that so exercised other political thinkers? He accepted the ancient view that the existence of parties and factions would be detrimental for establishing the general will:

> If citizens had no communication between each other while a sufficiently well-informed public deliberated, the general will would always become apparent, in spite of a great number of small differences, and the deliberation would always be good. . .It is therefore essential, if

the general will is to be able to make itself known, that there should be no partial society in the state and that each citizen should express only his own opinion: which was indeed the sublime and unique system established by the great Lycurgus.[83]

Despite his espousal of the public assembly as the means of creating laws, Rousseau was deeply suspicious of public deliberation and he expressed his deep hostility for the Athenian model of deliberation, warning about the danger that the citizens will be,

> seduced by private interests, which the credit of eloquence of some clever persons substitutes for those of the state: in which case the general will will be one thing, and the result of public deliberation another. This is not contradicted by the case of Athenian democracy; for Athens was not in fact a democracy, but rather a very tyrannical aristocracy, governed by scholars and orators.[84]

In Rousseau's view, the individual wills of the citizens were already formed when the assembly took place; the voting had merely the purpose of finding out what the general will is. In such circumstances, deliberation proper would only ensure the corruption of citizens by clever speakers. Rousseau made very clear that any view of the political activity which takes the will of the citizens as already formed, will end up being deeply suspicious about mass deliberation. Rousseau's legacy was deeply influential: with the help of ancient models he effectively invented the idea of political culture. And his views on virtue and the danger of parties would soon play an important role during the French Revolution.

The French Revolution, in its first stages, had little use for antiquity. When, however, the country found itself in a life or death combat with all European monarchies and was forced to suspend the king from his duties and ultimately execute him and abolish monarchy, new issues came to the forefront. The establishment of the republic, governed by an assembly which effectively combined both legislative and executive power, and the fighting of the war in circumstances of chaos and scarcity put again at the forefront the issue of virtue. Virtue was necessary if citizens were to sacrifice their lives to defend their country; it was essential if citizens were to put the common good above their personal interest and help the state instead of hoarding and profiteering; it was necessary if politicians were to steer the right course for the endangered republic. In these circumstances, antiquity became a crucial source of inspiration and guidance.[85] The French National Convention adorned its assembly room with statues of Solon, Lycurgus, Plato, Demosthenes, Camillus, Publicola, Brutus and Cincinnatus.[86] The writings of Rousseau and Mably, which presented the ancient republics of Sparta and Rome as exemplary communities, because their virtuous citizens were ready to sacrifice private interest in the altar of the common good, exerted widespread influence among political actors who desperately needed evidence that their own struggle was not hopeless. The Jacobin leader Maximilienne Robespierre phrased this quest in an exemplary manner:

> What is the principle of democratic or popular government, the essen-tial spring that maintains it and moves it? It is virtue; I speak of the public virtue which produced so many marvels in Greece and Rome, and which must produce far more astonishing ones in republican France; of that virtue which is nothing more than love of the *patrie* and of its laws.[87]

But it was not simply a matter of models of virtue. Following Rousseau, who was inspired by ancient examples to propose institutions which would inculcate virtue and patriotism in the citizen body, the revolutionaries considered a wide range of such proposals. To give one example among many, Rabaut de Saint-Étienne, one of the most classicising deputies, proposed to the Convention in 1792 the creation of 'temples nationales', which would be both school buildings and assembly halls, and in which citizens would gather every Sunday to participate in gymnastics, public games, military exercises and lectures on virtue.[88]

The Terror soon made clear one potential direction this view of virtue could take. If virtue was necessary for saving the republic from its enemies, then the community had the obligation to inculcate virtue in its citizens; action had to be taken to contain those citizens who were corrupted and put the republic in danger; finally, all parties and partial associations had to be suppressed to ensure that citizens followed only the general interest. The reaction to this discourse of virtue was slow in coming. Among the partisans of the Revolution, Camille Desmoulins, who eventually fell victim to the Terror, warned that virtue was not an adequate solution:

> If virtue was the only spring of government, if you suppose all men to be virtuous, the form of government is of no importance and all are equally good. Why, therefore, do we have some governments which are detestable and others that are good? Why do we have a horror of monarchy and cherish republics? It is, one supposes with reason, that men are not all equally virtuous, the goodness of the government must supplement virtue.[89]

In the aftermath of the Terror, there emerged a consensus that ancient political thought was responsible for the revolutionary excesses. Instead of the reliance on virtue and participation, the majority of contemporaries agreed that only the division of powers, representation and the pursuit of interest could be the modern answer to the problems of politics. The model of politics created by Montesquieu and the Federalists established itself as the new orthodoxy. One would have thought that after such a profound castigation of ancient politics there would be no way back. But such expectations soon proved unfounded. In the second half of the nineteenth century, many liberal thinkers expressed dissatisfaction with the limited scope for political action that the new orthodoxy posed. Instead, they came to stress the educative character of the political process.[90] It is characteristic that the model ancient polity was not any more Rome or Sparta, but Athens. The model citizen was not anymore the Roman and Spartan virtuous hero ready to sacrifice himself for his country, but the common Athenian citizen who

identified with the common good and educated himself through participating in political activity. The model text was no longer Plutarch or Livy,
but Thucydides' *Funeral Speech* and Demosthenes. It is within this context
of deliberation, public service and participation that Athens has exerted its
most significant influence on modern politics, rather than on the question
of rule we examined in chapter one. John Stuart Mill was one of the most
influential of these thinkers; in his work, he combined elements of the
Platonic and Aristotelian political philosophy with a deep admiration for
Athenian politics.[91] For Mill, the participatory character of Athenian democracy had an extremely important educative role. It allowed and encouraged
every citizen, no matter his economic or social background, to devote part
of his time to public affairs and thus to exercise his abilities.

> Notwithstanding the defects of the social system and moral ideas of
> antiquity, the practice of the dicastery and the ecclesia raised the
> intellectual standard of an average Athenian citizen far beyond
> anything of which there is yet an example in any other mass of men,
> ancient or modern.[92]

Even more, Mill stressed the importance of deliberation in Athenian
politics:

> The Athenian Constitution . . . had the additional democratic char-
> acteristic, far more practically important than even the political fran-
> chise; it was a government of boundless publicity and freedom of
> speech. It had the liberty of the bema, of the dicastery, the portico,
> the palæstra, and the stage; altogether a full equivalent for the liberty
> of the press . . . Enemies and friends alike testify that the parrhesia
> of Athens was paralleled in no other place in the known world. Every
> office and honour was open to every citizen, not, as in the aristo-
> cratic Roman republic (or even the British monarchy), almost nomi-
> nally, but really, while the daily working of Athenian institutions (by
> means of which every citizen was accustomed to hear every sort of

question, public and private, discussed by the ablest men of the time, with the earnestness of purpose and fulness of preparation belonging to actual business, deliberative or judicial) formed a course of political education, the equivalent of which modern nations have not known how to give even to those whom they educate for statesmen. . .The potency of Grecian democracy in making every individual in the multitude identify his feelings and interests with those of the state, and regard its freedom and greatness as the first and principal of his own personal concerns, cannot be better described than in the words of Mr. Grote.[93]

But Mill was also heavily influenced by the Platonic belief in the necessity of philosophers and experts in the conduct of public affairs. What is truly remarkable is his argument that in a direct democracy like Athens it was easier for philosophers and experts to exert their influence than in a modern representative system.[94]

The multitude have often a true instinct for distinguishing an able man, when he has the means of displaying his ability in a fair field before them. If such a man fails to obtain at least some portion of his just weight, it is through institutions or usages which keep him out of sight. In the old democracies there were no means of keeping out of sight any able man: the bema was open to him; he needed nobody's consent to become a public adviser. It is not so in a representative government; and the best friends of representative democracy can hardly be without misgivings, that the Themistocles or Demosthenes, whose counsels would have saved the nation, might be unable during his whole life ever to obtain a seat.[95]

Thus, Mill thought necessary the introduction of proportional representation and plural voting for the educated elite in order to guarantee the influence of the educated expert in the political process.

It would be an understatement to say that the twentieth century has been characterised by suffering and horror to a scale that was truly unprecedented. For many political thinkers, in particular those of a liberal persuasion, the most baffling and threatening experience has been the rise of a new political phenomenon, which they called totalitarianism. Nazism and Stalinism were the most successful examples of this wider phenomenon. For these liberal thinkers, the phenomenon of totalitarianism presented two important facets: one was the use of mass political participation in order to destroy liberal democracies and substitute them with illiberal regimes. The other was the substitution of political activity and deliberation with a vision of political knowledge as providing the means of solving every political and social problem.

Liberal thinkers have argued that the vision of politics as a form of knowledge is one of the most dangerous constructions of political thought; and many of them have thought that ancient political thought has been a particularly damning influence in this respect. The most famous example came in the aftermath of World War II, when the Austrian philosopher Karl Popper blamed the political thought of Plato for providing a blueprint for the totalitarian regimes of Nazism and Stalinism.[96] The Platonic conception of politics posed a threat to what Popper called the open society. By identifying politics with a form of knowledge, it was possible to construct a blueprint for how a community should be organised, to suppress deliberation as unnecessary, and to create a nightmare by trying to put this blueprint into practice. Instead, for Popper, only piecemeal reform on the basis of the experimental model of the natural sciences and the exchange of views among scientists could provide any hope of change for the better.

On the other hand, many political scientists embraced apathy as a fundamental value in politics. For this school of thought, which has been called the elitist school, widespread participation creates the danger of extremists taking advantage and subverting constitutional regimes to create totalitarian states; this was, in their view, the lesson of the Russian Revolution and the Nazi rise to power. Thus, politics should be better restricted to the selection of rulers between competitive sections of the political elite. In this approach, politics is seen through the model of the market: the citizen is a consumer who essentially has to choose between different products offered by competitors.[97] The free choice of the citizen and the existence of political competition are the only checks that suffice to guarantee the system's legitimacy, stability and success.[98] This school of thought reigned supreme during the 50's and 60's and continues to have many adherents even today.

But many political thinkers and activists since the 50's have reacted against this dominant conception of politics and have tried to construct and disseminate alternative models. Many of them have found ancient political thought and practice an enormous asset in the process of constructing such an alternative approach. One of the most influential has been Hannah Arendt. Arendt reasserted the value of political activity on its own and attacked its conception as an instrumental means to other ends.[99] But she drew a significant distinction between ancient political practice (in particular Athens) and ancient political philosophy. For Arendt, the Athenian distinction between the private sphere of the *oikos* and the political space of the *agora* was emblematic of the fact that ancient politics were fundamentally divorced from social and economic concerns, which were essentially the concern of the *oikos*. The *agora* was the space where citizens deliberated and acted regarding the public concerns; where the citizen acquired a public self and achieved fame and glory for his deeds and words. This understanding of political activity is in direct contrast with the identification of politics with a form of knowledge, which we saw originating with Plato; and, in fact, Arendt engaged into a long argument against Plato and subsequent political philosophers, alleging that their understanding brings hierarchy and control into politics, instead of equality and exchange of argument.[100] Arendt's agonistic perception of politics has thus used ancient political practice as a model of what politics should be about. On the left side of the political spectrum, thinkers like Cornelius Castoriadis and Jacques Rancière have seen the Athenian conception of politics as offering a radical alternative for rethinking political activity in the modern world.[101]

Others have concluded that the liberal understanding of politics as the pursuit and balance of interests has led to the devaluation of political activity,

apathy and the domination of the political field by powerful special interests. According to these thinkers, who mainly identify themselves as communitarians,[102] in order to revitalise political activity and participation it is
necessary that citizens share a perception of the common good and culti-
vate certain civic virtues. Aristotelian political philosophy is crucial in these
modern explorations: Aristotle's famous description of man as a political
animal is used in order to defend the thesis that participation in political
activity is an essential aspect of what it means to be human; his account
of the virtues and the common good is used to support the claim that the
political community needs to educate its citizens into developing certain
civic virtues and a shared perception of the common good which are essential for the proper functioning of every political community.[103] While it is
fascinating to see how Aristotle can still inspire modern thinkers, it is equally
interesting to note how modern thinkers who adopt his theory of citizenship and virtue tend to miss the ambiguity of Aristotle's reaction to political activity and misconstrue him as a communitarian with a unitary concept
of community. In fact, a few thinkers have even argued that the value of
Aristotelian political philosophy for modern times lies rather in his recognition of the inevitability of disagreement and conflict in normal human
communities and his defence of the shared medium of speech as the means
of achieving any common end.[104]

Some thinkers have seen in Athenian democracy an example which
disproves the elitist assumption that mass participation can only lead to
disaster and that any stable and successful political system must be led by
an elite. The wave of radicalisation that was spawned by the French student
revolt of May 68 and lasted until the late 70s made the idea of mass political participation popular again with many activists and theorists. M. I.
Finley, the most influential ancient historian of the twentieth century,
published a book that argued that the historical evidence showed that
mass popular participation in running the state had led to a stable and
fairly successful political system.[105] Josiah Ober, another influential ancient
historian, has argued that the example of Athens disproves Michels' iron
law of oligarchy, which states that in every political system an oligarchy

is always lurking behind the façade. Popular control of public rhetoric ensured that elite politicians were not able to transform into a ruling oligarchy.[106] More recently, Ober has also suggested that mass political participation in Athenian democracy created its own grassroots model of knowledge, which is superior to top-down models where decisions are taken by experts.[107]

I shall finish this chapter with a few comments on normative issues. We have seen the various ways in which Greek and Roman reflection and practice on the issue of political activity has influenced the modern world. But there are certainly still many ways in which ancient political theory and practice can illuminate our problems and help us solve them. Let me give two examples, one as illumination and one as solution, both from the field of deliberation. We have seen how many thinkers, from antiquity until the present, have struggled to tackle the problems created by mass deliberation. Overwhelmingly, modern thinkers have followed their ancient ancestors in being deeply suspicious of mass deliberation, as we saw above. But one of the most recent developments in political philosophy is an attempt to defend deliberation from its critics. Deliberative democracy, as this approach is called, has its origins in Jürgen Habermas' theory of communicative action and discourse ethics.[108] Its advocates argue that deliberative democracy can enhance the legitimacy of the democratic process by fostering wider citizen participation and devising rules that can allow discussants to reach a rational consensus on public issues. In contrast to the widespread suspicion of mass deliberation, which we have encountered in many of the political thinkers we have examined, deliberative democrats stress the possibilities created by the deliberative process. Despite the obvious attractions of the theory, there are many important drawbacks, and its proponents could benefit a lot by paying closer attention to ancient political thought and practice. It is illuminating to note that their model of rational dialogue was invented by Plato as a *counter* to democratic deliberation. Its purpose was to improve the participants by making them reexamine their assumptions and to show the absurdity of majority voting.

Rational dialogue was not invented to reach decisions, but to defer making them until one is certain about what one knows; thus it is ill-fitted as a model for the political process.[109] Academics never ask their audience to vote whether they were convinced after giving a paper, because their purpose is to discover the 'truth', not to reach a decision. The attempt to found deliberation on rationality, historically, leads away from, rather than towards democratic politics; the attempt to formulate safe rules of discussion, or the hope of an ultimate consensus, is inspired by a logic which is inherently problematic.

If we cannot base deliberation on rationality, is there any other way deliberation can be saved? It seems to me that the Athenians provided one long ago. It is impressive how little we have reflected on the Athenian practice of accountability for political advice and decision-making.[110] To give a recent example, in 2003, George W. Bush and Tony Blair instigated an invasion of Iraq against widespread popular opposition to the war in both of their countries and without UN sanction. In the aftermath, they have both admitted that the evidence on which the invasion was publicly justified was spurious, if not fraudulent. The war has led to thousands of dead civilians and combatants, an internecine civil war, the destruction of a country's infrastructure and cultural heritage, the wider destabilisation of the area, the expansion of terrorist activities and a huge financial drain on the invading countries in circumstances of deepening economic crisis. And yet, the possibility that these political leaders will ever give account for their proposals, decisions and actions is rather unlikely, despite the enormous havoc they have created. Modern political systems contain provisions of accountability only in circumstances in which the law has been definitively breached. The Athenian system, in which speakers and magistrates were also deemed responsible for their proposals and actions, could not be more different. Is there nothing left in it, from which we can profit?

CHAPTER IV

THE ENDS OF POLITICS: THE GOOD LIFE, A BETTER WORLD

We have come to the final part of our exploration. What were the aims of politics according to the Greeks and the Romans and how have their answers influenced the modern world? We can start with a very simple observation. The answer to this question cannot be independent from an account of man as a species and of men in their associations. It is the answer to this wider question which determined what the ancients had to say about the ends of politics. A first answer, which exerted enormous influence in the course of antiquity, is that the aim of man is to achieve glory, bliss and a good reputation while alive and fame among his descendants when dead. One can find this perspective as early as Homer and it is still dominant in much later times.[1] We have seen how service to the community was seen as an avenue that an individual could follow and, by pursuing the common good, achieve glory, bliss and fame. The aim of politics is to provide individuals with the opportunity to achieve these. Thus, one of the most lasting legacies of antiquity concerns the ways it has linked the pursuit of the good life, or the construction of a better world, with politics. Many other civilisations have flourished without making this linkage.

The most influential expression of this wider Greek view of the purpose of politics took form in Aristotle's *Ethics* and *Politics*. For Aristotle, human beings, like all natural entities, have a purpose in life: to fulfil their end by achieving happiness and excellence in what makes them most human. To achieve excellence and happiness, human beings need both resources and relationships with other human beings which will allow them to perform to the best of their abilities and fulfil their needs. Community is essential for humans to achieve happiness and excellence. Human communities, from the smallest to the largest, take the form of associations between individuals: families, cult groups, armies, trade partnerships. The political community is the largest association which encompasses all smaller and partial associations. In contrast to partial associations, which aim only at a particular good, only the political community can provide individuals with the full range of resources, relationships and opportunities to achieve their ends.[2] For Aristotles the purpose of politics is not merely a covenant to guarantee that men do not injure and cheat each other. Every alliance or contract is about this, but the political community, while certainly playing this role as well, exists for a higher purpose: the moral perfection of its members through the development of their capacities.[3]

> Man is by nature a political animal; and so even when men have no need of assistance from each other they none the less desire to live together. At the same time, they are also brought together by common interest, so far as each achieves a share of the good life. The good life then is the chief aim of the political community, both collectively for all its members and individually.[4]

Aristotle provided a final expression of a conception of the aims of the political community that was widely shared and much older; and this view of the aim of politics opened up the possibility of a radical innovation. If the purpose of the political community was to provide its members with the opportunities for excellence and happiness, then one could construct an ideal community which would do so in a perfect or ideal manner. Perhaps the most influential invention of antiquity was the concept of the ideal community. Many communities over time were admired or respected for their power, success or stability; but it was only during the fifth century BCE that one of them emerged as an ideal community whose features, institutions and practices were seen as normative and imitable by other communities: this was of course Sparta.[5] It was long known that Sparta was a very powerful and respectable Greek community, which owed her success and happiness to the legislation introduced by the mythical lawgiver Lycurgus at some point in the distant past. It was also known that Sparta had some very distinct customs and institutions, which differentiated her from other Greek communities, and which were again attributed to Lycurgus. But it was only at the end of the fifth century BCE that Sparta emerged as an ideal community. This, as far as we know, took place in Athens. It was the critics of Athenian democracy and society who invented what has come to be called 'the Spartan mirage'. We can start our exploration with a crucial passage from Xenophon, a fourth-century Athenian author who wrote a very influential account of the Spartan polity:

> And yet another point may well excite our admiration for Lycurgus. It had not escaped his observation that communities exist where those who are willing to make virtue their study and delight fail somehow in ability to add to the glory of their fatherland. That lesson the legislator laid to heart, and in Sparta he enforced, as a matter of public duty, the practice of virtue by every citizen... And was this not a noble enactment, that whereas other states are content to inflict punishment only in cases where a man does wrong against his neighbour, Lycurgus imposed penalties no less severe on him who openly neglected to make himself as good as possible?... Moreover, he laid upon them, like some irresistible necessity, the obligation to cultivate the whole virtue of a citizen. Provided they duly performed the injunctions of the law, the city belonged to them, each and all, in absolute possession and on an equal footing. Weakness of limb or lack of property was no drawback in his eyes.[6]

Virtue was necessary for the well-being of every political community. But virtue was constantly endangered by corruption. The Spartan solution, instituted by Lycurgus, was that the political community created and supervised a number of institutions and practices that aimed to ensure that citizens would be able and willing to learn and practice virtue. These institutions and practices included a system of public education in which all citizens, irrespective of birth and wealth, were obliged to participate; common messes; sumptuary legislation concerning personal expenditure; and the regulation of many aspects of social life, including marriage and sex.[7] The attempt to make the citizens virtuous through political intervention had one important consequence: it created a society of relatively equal conditions, in which birth and wealth did not wholly determine a citizen's standing in the community. The common experience of public education, the restrictions in the use of wealth and the common feasts created an atmosphere of equality: the Spartan citizens were known as the *homoioi*, the 'similars'.[8] Finally, we should note that the radical transformation of the Spartan community and her institutions were early on attributed to Lycurgus, a wise and virtuous lawgiver.

This image of Sparta had a profound effect on Greek political thought.[9] For our purposes, the most important case was the political thought of Plato. The pursuit of virtue and justice were fundamental values in the whole of the Platonic corpus. As he put it, politics 'is an art whose task is caring for the souls'.[10] In order to understand Plato's approach to the aims of politics, we need to acknowledge a fundamental break in his perspective in the course of his intellectual life.[11] Early Platonic dialogues were based on the image of Socrates trying to guide and educate his co-citizens in the pursuit of justice and virtue through discussion and the elenctic method. According to Socrates, virtue was knowledge: nobody was wicked willingly and thus discussion could illuminate the citizens and make them virtuous. But the fact that, in all these early dialogues, Socrates's interlocutors refused to be convinced and reformed, suggested that there was something fundamentally wrong with Socrates's initial premise. Plato introduced a different premise, which found its most fundamental expression in the *Republic*. This is the theory that the soul is tripartite, consisting of reason, spirit and desire. A person was just and virtuous when reason ruled over passion and desire, and the same applied to the community as a whole; but when desire, or the warlike spirit, ruled in an individual's soul or in a city, then one would find injustice, decadence and corruption. Reasoned discussion could only work for those people who have trained themselves to follow reason; for the rest, it was completely useless. Thus, only radical reform of the institutions of a corrupted community could ensure justice and virtue: in order to achieve a just and virtuous community, it was necessary either to educate the citizens from the time of their birth, or to radically reform the institutions of the community. This idea of radical moral reform is one of the most potent contributions of Plato to the history of political thought. The ideal community is for the first time something that can be constructed by political means.

It is at this point that the image of Sparta comes to play a fundamental role in Plato's construction of his ideal city.[12] This did not mean that Plato approved of everything in Sparta; but Sparta provided him with a template to use for constructing his own ideal community. The image of Lycurgus, a wise lawgiver who secures political power in order to implement a radical reform of the institutions and practices of a community, enabled Plato to conceive of his philosopher-kings: wise and virtuous individuals, who, if they would come to power, would be able to radically transform their communities and implement a just and virtuous regime. Spartan public education provided Plato with a model of the system of education that was necessary in order to achieve a virtuous community. But it is the sumptuary legislation and the regulation of social life in Sparta which furnished Plato with the most memorable innovation of the Republic: its revolutionary reorganisation of property and family. Plato was adamant that the moral education of the rulers was necessary but not sufficient. The exercise of power has always the potential to corrupt. Thus, it was necessary to form the life of the rulers in such a way that they would have no motive to misuse their power. The abolition of private property and the strict restriction in the use of wealth were necessary to ensure that the rulers would remain virtuous. The abolition of the nuclear family would ensure that birth and favouritism would play no role either.

Plato's suggestions were misinterpreted at the time he expressed them, and this misinterpretation had a profound influence on the development of ancient and modern political thought. Plato's provisions about family and property concerned only the ruling class of the Guardians and not the whole of the citizen body, as would happen with modern models of ideal communities. And while many later thinkers thought that Plato proposed the community of property, in fact he only suggested the abolition of private property: the Guardians would possess no property at all, apart from a few personal items, and they would be remunerated by the rest of the citizens through a tax.[13] Thus, Plato did not introduce the idea of the abolition of private property because he valued equality or community of property per se. It was only a means to ensure the preservation of something inherently valuable: virtue. But as we shall see, over time the Platonic proposal about property would be dissociated from its original context and would play a fundamental role of its own in political thought. His most important intentional contribution nevertheless was the description of a programme of radical reform by means of political power.

The image of Sparta would undergo one last important modification in the course of antiquity.[14] For reasons which historians still debate, Spartan society had changed significantly in the course of the fourth century BCE.[15] Many ancient authors thought that it was the result of the Spartan decision to allow the use of gold in their city, after their victory over the Athenians in the Peloponnesian War. Others believed that it was the result of a new law, which allowed citizens to freely bequeath their property, leading to wide-scale concentration of property in a few hands.[16] Whichever was the case, many thought that at the heart of the problem was corruption and luxury, which undermined the traditional Spartan order. In particular, after its defeat at Leuctra in 371 BCE, and its loss of Messenia in the following years, Sparta also lost her military vigour together with her frugality and relative social equality.

By the middle of the third century BCE, Sparta was a strongly class-divided society, where most of the land belonged to a few wealthy families. In the last decades of the third century, a Spartan king, Agis, attempted to radically change the situation. His plan was to cancel existing debts, to confiscate all land and to distribute an equal plot of land to each Spartan citizen. Agis's plans encountered strong opposition from the propertied and he was finally executed by the Spartan authorities. His work was taken over by king Cleomenes, who had married Agis's wife and was converted to his programme by her. Cleomenes also attempted to implement the redistribution of land in equal plots, but in the end was overthrown by the Macedonians and forced into exile.[17] What is important from our point of view is that, in order to defend their policies, Agis and Cleomenes claimed that their reforms were nothing more than a reintroduction of the laws of Lycurgus, which had fallen into abeyance. Nobody had ever previously claimed that there was equality of property in classical Sparta.[18] But now the idea emerged that Sparta was a society of strict equality in the division of property.

The Roman equivalent to Agis and Cleomenes took the form of the agrarian laws proposed by Tiberius Gracchus and his brother Caius in the late second century BCE.[19] By that time, many Roman citizens had become landless and a huge amount of land was concentrated in the hands of a tiny elite. The solution fostered by the Gracchi was the setting of an upper limit of 500 *jugera* for holdings of *ager publicus*, and the redistribution of the land in excess of this limit to the landless citizens. The *ager publicus* was public land confiscated from defeated enemies, which, with the passage of time, had effectively become private property. Although there was a limit to the amount of public land an individual could hold, in practice, by the late second century, some rich citizens had managed to acquire vast tracts. The Gracchan reforms largely failed, due to the ruthless opposition of the senatorial aristocracy, who had no qualms about murdering both brothers in order to maintain its wealth and privileges.

It was Plutarch, writing around 100 CE, who put together Platonic philosophy, the Spartan stories of Lycurgus, Agis and Cleomenes and the Roman example of the Gracchi in his *Parallel Lives*. In his *Life of Lycurgus* he presented an analysis of the principles of Lycurgus' legislation together with a memorable account of the institutions and practices he created. This account would prove enormously influential in later centuries, because it was the only text, which survived the Renaissance and beyond, presenting

Sparta as based on equality of property. Plutarch presented Lycurgus' legislation thus:

> A second, and a very bold political measure of Lycurgus, is his redistribution of the land. For there was a dreadful inequality in this regard, the city was heavily burdened with indigent and helpless people, and wealth was wholly concentrated in the hands of a few. Determined, therefore, to banish insolence and envy and crime and luxury, and those yet more deep-seated and afflictive diseases of the state, poverty and wealth, he persuaded his fellow-citizens to make one parcel of all their territory and divide it up anew, and to live with one another on a basis of entire uniformity and equality in the means of subsistence, seeking pre-eminence through virtue alone, assured that there was no other difference or inequality between man and man than that which was established by blame for base actions and praise for good ones.[20]

Lycurgus's reform of property relationships was a solution by political means to a number of social problems that bedevilled Spartan society. But the main emphasis in Plutarch is on the fact that the equality of property solved a very important political problem. Political pre-eminence was not based anymore on birth or wealth, but on the virtue that every citizen displayed in his services to the community. The equalisation of property was the best guarantee that the community would be ruled by the truly virtuous. We should, nevertheless, note that in Plutarch's account of the Gracchan reforms there is preserved a famous speech of Tiberius Gracchus, describing the appalling social conditions in Italy of his time, which points to a different justification of the agrarian law than the one offered by Plutarch himself:

> The wild beasts that roam over Italy, have, every one of them, a cave or lair to lurk in; but the men who fight and die for Italy enjoy the common air and light, indeed, but nothing else; houseless and home-

less they wander about with their wives and children. And it is with lying lips that their imperators exhort the soldiers in their battles to defend sepulchres and shrines from the enemy; for not a man of them has an hereditary altar, not one of all these many Romans an ancestral tomb, but they fight and die to support others in wealth and luxury, and though they are styled masters of the world, they have not a single clod of earth that is their own.[21]

Thus, Tiberius justified the agrarian law on the basis of need and desert, at least of those poor citizens who had served the commonwealth by fighting its wars. As such, this perspective is largely isolated in ancient political thought. Few, if any, ancient thinkers ever argued that the poor deserved, or had a right to, the redistribution of resources because of their need. But this isolated element would prove of great importance in modern times.

The importance of the ancient agrarian laws does not stop here. They were also instrumental in the creation of a very different conception of the aims of politics and the political community. This is the conception presented in the works of Cicero. Cicero was a profound critic of the agrarian laws and any similar legislation:

> But they who pose as friends of the people, and who, for that reason, either attempt to have agrarian laws passed, in order that the occupants may be driven out of their homes, or propose that money loaned should be remitted to borrowers, are undermining the foundations of the commonwealth; first of all they are destroying harmony, which cannot exist when money is taken away from one party and bestowed on another; and second, they do away with equity, which is utterly subverted, if the rights of property are not respected.[22]

But Cicero was able to present his opposition to agrarian laws within a wider argument about politics. According to him, the primary aim of politics is not to improve citizens or educate them in virtue; instead, the purpose of forming political communities was the protection of private property:

> For the chief purpose in the establishment of political communities and citizenships was that individual property rights might be secured. For, although it was by nature's guidance that men were drawn together into communities, it was in the hope of safeguarding their possessions that they sought the protection of cities.[23]

In other works, Cicero also added advantage (*utilitas*) and security as supreme aims of the political community; in contrast to Aristotle and Plato, where the political community had a positive aim, for Cicero the purpose of the state is rather negative: the protection of individuals and their possessions from external and internal enemies.[24] As we shall see, this account of the purpose of politics would be highly influential in later times.

The moderns

The rediscovery of classical texts during the Renaissance presented early modern Europeans with a number of subjects in terms of thinking about the ends of politics. Ancient political thought bequeathed to early modern Europeans an important assumption. The problems that bedevil human communities are the result of intentional human action and can be identified as such; consequently, intentional human action can be used in order to fight these evils, achieve the good life and create a better world. Therefore, the aim of political activity is to intervene in human interactions in order to arrange them in a better way and fight against the problems that bedevil them. Corruption, vanity, luxury, poverty and domination are the results of human passions, and politics can be used to fight against them, or even eliminate them altogether. The ancient assumption that the political community had the obligation to educate its citizens and make them just and virtuous was thus widely shared. But, among this wider consensus, ancient political thought provided two more extreme perspectives. The one was what a modern historian has recently called 'the Greek tradition'.[25] This was the Platonic-Plutarchean view that it was legitimate for the political community to redistribute property through agrarian and inheritance laws and curb luxury through sumptuary laws, in order to ensure that the community was ruled by the truly virtuous and not by the wealthy and powerful. The agrarian laws of Sparta and Rome played a particularly important role as models of how a political community had ensured the rule of virtue in the past. On the other hand, the writings of Cicero and the other attackers of the agrarian laws could be used to define a more circumscribed scope for political action, aiming at security of property and peace, rather than improvement and reform.

The history of ancient communities presented the moderns with a pattern of the effect of social ills on politics. The history of Sparta, Rome and, to a lesser extent, Athens illustrated the problems and the prospects modern societies faced. Second, ancient history provided possible solutions for curing modern evils, in the shape of agrarian or sumptuary laws, educational programmes etc. Third, ancient political thought and practice provided a means and a set of examples of how to think about and effect political reform. It was, in particular, the image of the ancient lawgiver, which proved enormously influential for early modern thinkers. The virtuous individual who manages to assume power and rearrange the political and social order captured the imagination of early modern thinkers. Lycurgus was the lawgiver par excellence; but he was joined by figures like Numa, Solon, the Gracchi, Agis and Cleomenes. It was Machiavelli who in his search for a model of radical political reform made ancient legislators a main staple of modern political reflections.[26]

The Platonic solution to the construction of the good society came to the fore in early modern Europe with the publication in 1516 of Thomas More's *Utopia*.[27] More presented Utopia as espousing Plato's proposals for radical reconstruction;[28] but, while assimilating many elements of Plato's model, he also innovated in two important ways. As we saw, Plato had only argued for the negation of property for the Guardians, while accepting the existence of private property for the rest of the citizens; but More presented a community in which private property was completely abolished and everything, with the exception of women and children, was shared in common. The reason was that More's community did not merely aim to guarantee the rule of the virtuous and the abolition of conflict; it also intended to provide all its members with the opportunity to work and procure the means of subsistence, in contrast to More's contemporary societies, which were characterised by widespread criminality, vagrancy and destitution. Such concerns were almost completely absent from ancient political thought, with the exception of the speech of Tiberius Gracchus we mentioned earlier.

Utopia inaugurated a long tradition of works identifying the ideal community, normally in some distant place.[29] Community of property, the absence of conflict, and the rule of the wise were instigated in many of these utopias. We tend to enquire about the means that these utopian works employed to affect such radical change and create a better world. But the early modern utopian tradition was largely uninterested in this question; it presented the *optimus reipublicae status* as already established in some distant place, and it usually did not enquire about the means through which it was originally established. The main purpose of this utopian tradition, therefore, was not the actual creation of a perfect community, but moral judgement on the ills of human communities.[30] The utopian models were mainly standards by which modern communities could be measured and judged, not blueprints for practical action.[31]

While More moved the Platonic-Plutarchean tradition in a fresh direction, other early modern thinkers put the stress on its traditional focus. James Harrington is the paradigmatic example of this tradition in modern times. We have seen how his magnum opus, the *Oceana*, was presented as the work of a great lawgiver, in an effort to convince Cromwell to play the role of Lycurgus. We have also seen Harrington's fundamental view that power follows property. According to this view, a Commonwealth could be established in England only because changes in the property regime had brought the largest part of land in the possession of the Commons. Thus, it was necessary to ensure that land was not again concentrated in the hands of few, for that would undermine the regime and bring an aristocracy into power. But it was also the case that inordinate wealth made impossible the choice of the wise and virtuous for political office and instead promoted the rich. To face these potential challenges, Harrington advocated the introduction of an agrarian law that would limit the amount of land an individual could possess and acquire.[32] With Harrington, Sparta came back to European political thought not only as a model of the mixed constitution, but also as a model political community due to its social structure.

Another good illustration of the link between the aim of politics, the agrarian laws and the image of the lawgiver is the most popular political and moral work of the whole eighteenth century, *The Adventures of Telemachus*, written by the French bishop Fénelon and published in 1699 without his authorisation.[33] Fenelon was tutor to Louis of France, Duke of Burgundy, the successor to the French throne, who, however, died before succeeding his grandfather Louis XIV. *Telemachus* was written as a work of advice to his pupil. The work took the form of a fictional sequel to the Odyssey. In the course of his travels to find Ulysses, Telemachus visits many communities, giving the opportunity to Fénelon to present the problems that bedevil communities and the ways these problems could be solved. Salentum, a community reformed by a wise lawgiver, proved a highly influential model in Enlightenment Europe.[34] Sumptuary and agrarian laws were used to destroy luxury and instil frugality and public spirit. Until Fénelon, the model of political intervention through the means of a wise lawgiver in order to create a better world reigned supreme. Of course, few people believed that radical reform could ever take place and the question of how such a wise lawgiver could ever assume power was not easily answered; but what was widely shared was the view that the political community and its rulers had an obligation to intervene in human affairs to ensure that citizens would be just and virtuous and the common good would be achieved. Decadence, a main concern in Fénelon's work, was not a mere personal trait of individuals, but a moral failure of citizens which affected the political community and about which the political community had an obligation to act.[35]

*

But even during the seventeenth century and increasingly in the eighteenth, the wider consensus that the aim of the political community was to improve its citizens broke down. The main catalyst was the religious wars between Catholics and Protestants that divided Europe during this period. The breakup of homogeneous religious and moral communities had significant effects on the understanding of politics. Some thinkers saw that the state claim to morally improve its citizens could easily lead to persecutions of the religious minorities; furthermore, the religious schism put severe strains on achieving any consensus on what the common good could mean. The creation of theories of natural rights and social contracts was an attempt to find a solution in a world whose shared conceptions were shattered.[36] These thinkers argued that political agreement could only be reached if the aims of the political community were restricted. The aim of politics should not be the moral formation of citizens, the pursuit of the common good, or the creation of conditions for the attainment of glory and the exercise of virtue; instead, politics had only the instrumental role of securing the natural rights of citizens. The right to self-preservation was seen as the most fundamental natural right, but the right to property was seen as emanating out of this fundamental right. It is obvious that this discourse was diametrically opposed to political intervention to redistribute property or educate the citizens for wider political aims. Cicero, who had argued that the purpose of the state was the protection of property, had thus returned to centre stage.

At the end of the seventeenth century and even more so in the eighteenth the ancient conceptions on the aims of politics received a further severe blow. From antiquity until the eighteenth century the standard models of human community were holistic and volitional. The modern distinctions between society, economy and the state did not exist. The Aristotelian view of the polis as an association aiming at the common good, encompassing and incorporating various other associations aiming at more specific goods, was still the dominant model. As we have seen, this model put a great emphasis on the intentional actions of the citizens: the various associations and the political community at large were maintained only because the citizens upheld justice and practiced virtue. It was thus necessary, for the attainment of the common good and the maintenance of stability, that the political community ensured that citizens were just and virtuous. The greatest innovation of the eighteenth century was the discovery of an alternative conception of human community which was neither holistic, nor volitional. It was not holistic, because it proposed a separation between the three distinct fields of the state, the economy and society. And it was not volitional, because it supported the idea that a community could function properly no matter the intentions of the people who made it up; in a more elaborate version, a human community was like a mechanical system which followed certain laws of its own, without having an intentional prime mover.

The discovery of this ingenious conception took place within the English debate on virtue and corruption. We have seen how opponents of the Court Whigs, after the Glorious Revolution of 1688, created a discourse of corruption to fight against the abuses of the system. In their view, a corrupt court which spread luxury and effeminacy, together with placemen, an extensive national debt, paper money, financial speculation and standing armies were intent on destroying the remnants of liberty and virtue in Britain and establish an absolute monarchy. The supporters of the Court needed to find a way of defending the new status quo. Against the charges of corruption, they came to argue that the intentions of individuals did not matter, as long as there was a system which could turn 'private vices into public benefits'.[37] The first salvo in this battle came with Bernard Mandeville's famous work *The Fable of the Bees* (1714). Mandeville argued that virtue was not necessary for a healthy polity; in fact, it was the unintended consequence of private vices which made it possible for society to function properly. The endpoint of this process was the emergence of what the French historian Pierre Rosanvallon has termed 'utopian capitalism'.[38] The market provided the basis of an auto-regulated society; an automatic mechanism that had no need of external intervention or the intentional action of a ruling authority to ensure the proper function of society and the satisfaction of its members' needs and wishes. As Adam Smith famously put it,

It is not from the benevolence of the butcher, the brewer, or the baker, that we expect our dinner, but from their regard to their own interest. We address ourselves, not to their humanity but to their self-love, and never talk to them of our own necessities but of their advantages. Nobody but a beggar chooses to depend chiefly upon the benevolence of his fellow-citizens.[39]

The functioning of previous societies was based on hierarchic relationships: that of ancient societies on slaves and masters, that of medieval societies on lords and serfs. But a market society could provide services and goods without hierarchy: it was a balanced system without a centre. Defending this new conception of society necessitated a ferocious attack on ancient polities. As we have seen in the previous chapter, there emerged a wholly new vision of ancient societies, as based on slavery, agriculture and warfare; in contrast, modern societies depended on free labour, commerce and the market. The ancient communities played a significant role as fodder in the efforts to defend the modern society of the market. In this conception, the sphere and aims of politics were severely circumscribed; not only was political action unnecessary for solving the problems of the community, but, on the contrary, political action could end up distorting or destroying the proper functioning of the market. As the American revolutionary Thomas Paine characteristically put it in 1776, the same year Smith's *Wealth of Nations* was published, 'society in every state is a blessing, but Government, even in its best state, is but a necessary evil'.[40] Perhaps the best expression of the non-volitional character of this new discourse was its attack on the image of the ancient lawgiver. Many thinkers came to dispute the historical existence of these mythical lawgivers. Instead they believed that those measures attributed to the ancient lawgivers were merely the expression of impersonal social processes and structures:

The reality, in the meantime, of certain establishments at Rome and at Sparta, cannot be disputed: but it is probable, that the government of both these states took its rise from the situation and genius

of the people, not from the projects of single men; that the celebrated warrior and statesman, who are considered as the founders of
those nations, only acted a superior part among numbers who were
disposed to the same institutions; and that they left to posterity a
renown, pointing them out as the inventors of many practices which
had been already in use, and which helped to form their own manners
and genius, as well as those of their countrymen.[41]

If the model of the market had unambiguous implications, the discourse
of natural rights was Janus faced. The reason was its radically egalitarian
premise. All human beings were seen as possessing the same natural rights
prior to entering into a contract to institute a political community. This
premise could lead to the rejection of a teleological account of human nature
and the human good. Every human being was morally equal to every other,
and thus should have an equal claim to determine what its own perception
of its good was. Thus, mainstream liberalism came to oppose strongly any
attempt to refashion human relationships in order to achieve a certain vision
of the good. On the other hand, it was possible to use nature and natural
rights as the foundation for projects to radically transform communities in
order to protect every person's natural rights and achieve social and political equality. As we shall shortly see, antiquity would play an important
role in turning this egalitarian reading of natural rights into a political
programme for implementation.

J. J. Rousseau was the most penetrating critic of contemporary societies
during the eighteenth century. Rousseau was completely unimpressed by
the arguments for the role of commerce and the market in creating a better
society. From the time man abandoned his natural state and entered into
society, his dependence on others and his *amour-propre* had transformed
him into the miserable creature that he was. The development of the arts
and the sciences had created inequality, had led to luxury and corruption
and hade made men more impotent. The only solution from this dependence and slavery was the artificial creation of an egalitarian polity to which
every man would direct his attention. The aim of politics cannot be merely

to fulfil the task of the night-watchman that liberal thinkers had confined it to. Rather, politics has the aim to educate and liberate the citizens.

> Make men, therefore, if you would command men: if you would have them obedient to the laws, make them love the laws, and then they will need only to know what is their duty to do it. This was the great art of ancient governments, in those distant times when philosophers gave laws to men, and made use of their authority only to render them wise and happy. Thence arose the numerous sumptuary laws, the many regulations of morals, and all the public rules of conduct which were admitted or rejected with the greatest care. . . But our modern governments, which imagine they have done everything when they have raised money, conceive that it is unnecessary and even impossible to go a step further.[42]

Rousseau was not content with pointing out the inherent contradictions of the human condition and the necessity of an artificial political intervention in order to denaturise men and to make them content and happy. The utopian thinkers before Rousseau had presented imaginary ideal communities which could function as standards by which one could judge modern communities. This, as we saw, was the reason that all these utopian thinkers were not really interested in the implementation of their utopian schemes, and, with the partial exception of Plato, had devoted no time in thinking about the actual means by which their utopias could be implemented.[43] This criticism could be turned to some extent against Rousseau as well.[44] But Rousseau presented a great innovation which would prove highly significant. In presenting historical communities, and in particular Sparta, as examples of what a happy and successful political community had been in the past, he succeeded in portraying social and political ills as specifically modern and thus historically surmountable: 'My opponents are visibly embarrassed every time Sparta is mentioned. What would they not give for this terrible Sparta never to have existed?'[45] Sparta was evidence that a different form of community was within the grasp of human beings and not mere idle dreaming.[46] Personally, Rousseau still clung to the image of the ancient lawgiver as the means of achieving radical political change; thus, he did not have great hopes that a radical transformation of human communities could be achieved. But the road was now open for others to find alternative means of bringing Sparta back to life in modern conditions.

The other man who had a significant role in making Sparta into a model for Enlightenment Europe was the French Abbé de Mably.[47] Mably was an adherent to the ancient principle that equality of property is a necessary precondition for the rule of the virtuous. Sparta was an exemplary case of this principle:

> What indeed availed the establishment of order, if avidity for riches, and its inseparable companion luxury, the sources of inequality among citizens, making some tyrants, others slaves, were suffered, by insensible degrees, to interrupt the harmony of the state? The populace, debased by indigence, too abject to dispute their supremacy, would have flattered the vanity of the great; and the reigning princes, augmenting the channels of corruption, would have panted for arbitrary power. In order to render his countrymen worthy of liberty, Lycurgus established a perfect equality of fortune.[48]

As with all previous thinkers, Mably did not propose a strict equality of property, but only the absence of wide disparities in property and the curbing of luxury and the use of wealth. But in the course of his intellectual development the agrarian laws as a guarantee of virtue was fused with the discourse of natural rights and the Utopian tradition that stemmed from Thomas More. Although Mably denounced the misery and poverty created by private property and argued in favour of a community of property, he was less interested in attempts to create such a society than in creating a virtuous political community. He was thus closer to the Plutarchean tradition than to the Utopian. But, in his debates with the physiocratic defenders of private property, he provided an important link between the two discourses.

Whereas previous thinkers had projected polities based on a community of goods in the primitive past or in far away places, Mably gave it a historical foundation by presenting Sparta in such a light. Until then, Sparta was seen as an egalitarian society where each citizen had an equal plot of land, which was, though, private property. But Mably argued against the physiocrats that there were communities without private property in land and Sparta was such a community, since the citizens had only the usufruct of the land, which belonged to the state.[49]

It was thus during, the eighteenth century, that the 'Greek tradition' of agrarian laws met with the defence of equality and the struggle to alleviate poverty.[50] Until the later eighteenth century, agrarian laws, sumptuary laws, community of property or state intervention were primarily supported for political reasons: to countervail the debilitating influence of wealth on merit, to secure a virtuous citizenry, and to ensure the patriotic attachment of the citizen soldiers. The equalisation of property was not fostered because poor citizens deserved more resources or because they needed them. The person who finally fused these two traditions into a new potent mix was the French revolutionary François-Noël Babeuf, who changed his Christian name to that of Gracchus, in order to honour the two Roman tribunes, supporters of the agrarian law.[51] On 13 March 1793, the French National Convention decreed that any proposal to implement an agrarian law would be punished by death.[52] In fact, the modern scientific study of Roman history which is associated with the name of the Danish statesman and historian Barthold Georg Niebuhr was the result of the agitation for an agrarian law. As Niebuhr stated, his work on Roman history, which was the first to present a modern narrative based on a scientific criticism of the sources, was sparked by the need to show that the modern proponents of an agrarian law had not read the ancient texts critically and had not understood that the Roman agrarian laws pertained only to the *ager publicus*, and not to the sacrosanct private property.[53]

But, with Babeuf, the agrarian law was no longer a means to effect the preservation of virtue, or the rule of the wise. Instead it was linked to equality and the natural rights of humanity. The ancient versions of the agrarian law had little to do with equality; but now Babeuf's slogan was 'loi agraire, égalité réelle' (agrarian law is the real equality). Babeuf argued that nature gave every human being an equal right to the enjoyment of wealth and that the aim of a political community was to defend this equality. Thus, he called for a political revolution in order to abolish private property, establish the community of goods, and create a happy society.[54] The Roman tribunes, according to Babeuf the champions of equality, provided him with a model of the organisation that was necessary to overthrow inequality and institute communism. Babeuf was the first to create a revolutionary organisation that would put into practice the radical reorganisation of society. In this respect he was the progenitor of the communist and socialist parties and other revolutionary groups of the nineteenth and twentieth centuries.

With Babeuf we arrive at a point in which a number of elements inherited from ancient political thought were transformed into something new. Plato's insistence on the need for political action in order to radically transform the community and solve its problems was wholly adopted; the agrarian laws of Sparta and Rome became instruments not for the rule of the wise and virtuous, but for the creation of an egalitarian society through the abolition of private property and the imposition of the community of goods. Finally, the problem of the means of radical reform was solved in a wholly new way. It was not any more the exceptional figure of the ancient lawgiver who would achieve such an aim; instead, it was the Roman tribunes, defenders of the people's interests, who provide the models for a revolutionary organisation that would overthrow the status quo and create the new world.

It is obvious that in Babeuf we see many of the elements that coalesced into the *Communist Manifesto*, published by Karl Marx and Friedrich Engels in 1848. Marxism, the most influential political philosophy of the last two centuries, is thus to an important extent a descendant of ancient political thought. We can see how the idea of radical reform of society through political means, the idea of the community of property as the solution to social and political problems and the idea of a revolutionary organisation all stemmed from ancient political thought. But there is another important element of Marx's thought which has an ancient pedigree. The most impressive difference between Marx and the long tradition which, stemming from Plato, envisages the creation of a perfect community, is Marx's constant unwillingness to provide an account of what his ideal community would look like. Most of the works in this tradition had tried to specify even the details of such ideal communities, while Marx always resisted this temptation. To understand why, we have to turn to the influence of Aristotle's view of the aim of politics.[55] Marx shared Aristotle's view that man is an animal that can only individuate itself in the midst of society. But, even more, he was influenced by Aristotle's claim about the purpose of the political community. The purpose of politics and the ideal community is not to prescribe the ideal form of life for its members; instead, it is to allow human beings to flourish and fulfil their potentialities as human beings. This is the reason that a detailed blueprint was seen as unnecessary.

But let us return to the time of the French revolution. It does not need much imagination to realise why in 1776, and even more in 1789, the image of the ancient lawgiver was of crucial importance.[56] In both cases legislators were entrusted with a task of leaving the past behind and designing their political communities anew; the image of the lawgiver was not only a means of understanding their position, but also of inspiring hope that they could succeed in their tasks. The Jacobin leaders of the French Revolution, in particular, used power not only to promote the reign of virtue through institutions like civic festivals, inspection of morals and generalised school education, but also by promoting policies of economic and social welfare; the Jacobin leader Saint-Just expressed the feeling of the radical change in the view of the aims of the political community by saying that 'happiness is a new idea in Europe'.[57] We have seen in the previous chapter how antiquity played an important role in inspiring and justifying these policies. But, after the fall of the Jacobins, the idea that politics should aim to reform and improve the community and the image of the lawgiver came under vicious attack. Antiquity and its Jacobin imitators were accused of trying to change the world by an act of will and thus going against the fundamental laws and structures that directed human communities. Social science, the discipline to study the new concept of society, was created by a group of French intellectuals called the *Idéologues*, after the fall of the Jacobins in 1794.[58] The *Idéologues* orchestrated a relentless attack on ancient polities and political thought; social science would be the antidote to ancient politics, by studying the laws of function and motion of society and suggesting policies that would be consistent with these laws. Ancient polities could not be recreated by an act of political will, and politics should be subservient to the rulings of social science.

Thus, in the aftermath of the revolution the conditions of employing antiquity in modern debates changed rapidly. The moderns, who argued that market society had no need any more of ancient recipes, held the day for a considerable time; in fact, this position has survived until the present, waging greater or lesser influence in different periods and countries. In the camp of those who argued for the necessity of political intervention, or the radical transformation of society, antiquity ceased to provide solutions that could be adopted in modern circumstances, like the agrarian or sumptuary laws; equally, antiquity ceased to provide a narrative of social change and revolution that could be used to understand the present and predict the future. Finally, the overthrow of the image of the lawgiver as an effective means of engineering social and political change meant that the ancient lawgivers ceased to provide a model for modern reformers and revolutionaries.

Be that as it may, even under these circumstances, antiquity did not cease to exert a profound influence on modern thinkers. Ancient political thought and practice became now a source of inspiration; it provided a means of criticising what was wrong in modern society; and it provided a means of reflection on the fundamental problems of effecting social and political change. The liberal laissez-faire approach did not last long. In the last decades of the nineteenth and the beginning of the twentieth century, it became obvious that the market was far from an auto-regulated system and that political intervention was necessary in order to alleviate the misery and poverty created by the development of industry and capitalism. This took place within a convergence, wherein some liberals abandoned their individualist and laissez-faire attitude and some socialists abandoned their revolutionary creed. Both groups were looking for a political philosophy that would enable them to find a political solution to the social problems of modern societies. Classical thought played an important role in providing these thinkers and activists with such a political philosophy. This was particularly the case in England, where Idealist thinkers like T. H. Green, who were influenced by Platonic and Aristotelian political and moral philosophy, played a key role in the intellectual and political process that led to the creation of the welfare state.[59] The image of the Greek polis provided these thinkers with an important argument about what a political community should be about. It allowed them to move beyond the liberal focus on the isolated individual and stress the importance of citizenship and the pursuit of the common good. This recognition of the moral function of the state was instrumental in supporting the claim that the state should intervene and allocate communal resources to achieve the welfare of every citizen.

Normative political theory seemed defunct in the middle decades of the twentieth century; but it returned to the fore with the publication in 1971 of John Rawls' *A Theory of Justice*.[60] While remaining within the liberal paradigm, Rawls attempted to present an idea of a just society together with the means that could be used to bring into life. Rawls carefully distinguished between a non-liberal full theory of the good, which prescribes what is good for humans, and a liberal thin theory of the good, which does not prescribe what human beings should aim at, but only delineates certain basic requirements for life, which every member of the society could reasonably agree under certain circumstances that they should be guaranteed to everybody.

Thus, Rawls attempted to justify an end for politics, while at the same time trying to avoid subscribing to a normative theory of the human good, like those of Plato and Aristotle that we have examined. There have been many different reactions to Rawls' thesis that modern political communities should remain neutral as regards conceptions of the common good and the best life.[61] Some of them are directly influenced by ancient political thought and in particular by Aristotle.[62] These thinkers have followed in the footsteps of Rawls and attempted to complement Rawls' account of justice with Aristotle's perspective on human fulfilment. Martha Nussbaum has been one of the most influential among these scholars.[63] She accepts the liberal premise that the state should not try to promote a particular version of the good life and that the moral equality of human beings dictates the equality of their choices. But in contrast to those who make the further premise that the state should be restricted to the role of the night-watchman, she argues that Aristotle's perspective of fulfilment as the end of human life can be used to construct a positive role for the political community. In order to be able to excel in whatever end one chooses for oneself, there are certain capabilities which are essential; the role of the political community is to ensure that every citizen has the resources and opportunities necessary to develop his capabilities. The Aristotle-inspired capabilities approach makes it possible for the political community to claim a positive role beyond that of the night-watchman, without obliging the political community to prioritise a particular perspective of the good life.

This example shows the persistent ability of ancient political thought to inspire modern reflections on the end of politics and the means of achieving them. But, as Eric Nelson has recently commented, liberal moral egalitarianism and the wish to create a better world, whether through advancing the fulfilment of capabilities, the performance of virtue, or the claims of justice, are inherently incompatible. We cannot square absolute moral egalitarianism and political intervention, because, given the plurality of views, any plan to use communal resources for some end will always go against some cherished views of some individual or a group. We have seen that moral egalitarianism and the hope to create a better world have indeed had different historical trajectories. So we are only left with the necessity to choose – and the moral and political responsibilities of our choice.[64]

EPILOGUE

Let us now finish this exploration with a few general conclusions and thoughts. My first observation is that history plays strange games, and it is these strange games which justify the joint discussion of Greek and Roman political thought, despite their significant differences. If it was the Greeks who invented a vocabulary of the different forms of political rule, to which the Romans were largely indifferent, it was nevertheless through the history of Rome that modern thinkers tested and explored the validity of this vocabulary until the nineteenth century. This was mainly because even in antiquity a Greek thinker, Polybius, had applied this Greek vocabulary to Roman politics. These strange games of history should also warn us against reading the history of political thought in an anachronistic manner. Until the late eighteenth century, discussions of democracy were largely focused on Rome and not, as many scholars have assumed, on Athens; it was only after this point that Athens emerged as the sole point of reference.

A second thing, which I hope has become clear to the reader, is that the history of the reception of ancient political thought is not linear. It is true that, from the Renaissance till the eighteenth century, ancient political thought and ancient history had both a normative and an explanatory power of major importance; it is also true, as we have seen time and again, that the period around the American and the French Revolutions constitutes an important turning point. The reception of ancient political thought has been significantly modified by the belief that these revolutions heralded the creation of modernity; in this new world antiquity could not anymore provide a pattern through which contemporary developments could be comprehended and future trajectories predicted. But it is this very irrelevancy of ancient politics in a modern society which has made ancient political thought a major weapon in the hands of all those wishing to fight against the evils of modernity, from Rousseau and Marx to Mill and Arendt. For these reasons, different aspects of ancient political thought have fared very differently over the centuries. If the question 'who should rule' has been largely discarded in the last fifty years, ancient models of political participation and deliberation have become particularly influential during the same period of time.

A third conclusion is that the reception of ancient political thought cuts across contemporary ideological distinctions between liberalism, republicanism, Marxism or conservatism. The often repeated distinction between republicans influenced by antiquity and liberals rejecting ancient political thought is both crude and misleading. Liberals could reject ancient political thought in certain respects and adopt it wholeheartedly in others, as the example of Mill shows; republicans like Harrington could use some elements of ancient political thought in order to discard some fundamental assumptions of ancient politics and construct a model of political action which was fundamentally compatible with liberal assumptions. The fear of power is a distinct feature of modern liberalism; but, while some thinkers expressed this fear through recourse to antiquity and by calls to civic vigilance, others identified ancient political thought as the very source of the danger they feared.

My fourth conclusion is that the relationship between ancient and modern political thought is complex and cannot be summarised with any simple statement. We have come across the enormous variety within ancient political thought and we have seen how different modern thinkers, or generations of thinkers, have appealed to different aspects of this variegated tradition. In fact, it can be argued that ancient political thought possesses a unity only in retrospective terms: only when we compare certain ancient ideas and viewpoints to certain modern ones is it possible to discover any underlying unity in ancient political thought. The presentation of ancient political thought as a coherent tradition has largely been the product of modern polemics: in some cases to find a suitable ally against a particular modern opponent, in others to construct a convenient opponent while asserting a particular modern point of view. No single and no simple distinction between ancient and modern political thought will sufficiently account for the complex process of adoption, transformation and contrast that we have traced in this book.

But, perhaps, there is an exception to the statement that ancient political thought does not possess any inherent element of unity. The twenty first-century reader should be in a better position to recognise this element than the twentieth-century one. This element is the assumption that the world of politics consists solely of human beings, their actions and their thoughts and does not necessitate the existence of a transcendental order and its claims on human beings. To put it more crudely, ancient political thought can be presented as a secular tradition which consciously excludes considerations of religion. There is little doubt that there is an important element of truth in this assertion; there is even less doubt that ancient political thought has indeed been treated by the moderns as a secular tradition, and has been valued and employed precisely because it made possible the construction of political arguments that defied the religious establishments, or denied the validity of religious concerns in political matters. Machiavelli was probably the first modern to consider ancient political thought in this light and was followed by innumerable others. From our current standpoint, when political arguments from transcendental sources are widely proclaimed in both East and West, the peculiarity of this tradition of political thought which starts with the Greeks and the Romans should not escape our attention.

But my intention is not to identify or praise the uniqueness of this tradition; instead, I wish to point out a final paradox. It is in fact possible to write the history of ancient political thought and its modern reception as the history of a secular tradition, as I have done it in this volume. And we should, in fact, evaluate both the deficiencies and the advantages of this secular tradition. But this is not the whole story. For one of the most fascinating chapters in the history of Greek and Roman political thought is how this secular tradition provided the materials and terms for the construction of one of the most influential non-secular political theories from antiquity till the present: namely the one constructed by Augustine in his *City of God*. The story of how the secular tradition of Greece and Rome has been interacting over the centuries with that initiated by Augustine remains still to be written. The Commonwealthmen of the English Revolution[1] and Rousseau[2] are merely the most famous examples of how the two different traditions could merge into one, in fascinating ways. Perhaps this can teach us something about our contemporary predicament. But it certainly testifies to the enormous complexity of Greek and Roman political thought and the multiplicity of ways in which it has shaped and will continue to shape the questions we ask and the answers we seek.

NOTES

Introduction

1 Quoted in Koselleck, Reinhard, *Futures Past. On the Semantics of Historical Time* (Massachusetts and London, 1985), p. 21.

2 Quoted in Vidal-Naquet, Pierre, 'The tradition of Greek democracy' *Thesis Eleven* 60 (2000), pp. 65–6.

3 Marx, Karl, 'The Eighteenth Brumaire of Louis Bonaparte' in Marx, Karl and Engels, Friedrich, *Collected Works: Vol. 11* (New York, 1979), p. 104.

4 For an important liberal version of this argument, see Holmes, Stephen T., 'Aristippus in and out of Athens', *American Political Science Review* 73 (1979), pp. 113–128.

5 Miller, Peter N., *Defining the Common Good. Empire, Religion and Philosophy in Eighteenth-Century Britain* (Cambridge, 1994).

6 Lane, Melissa S., *Plato's Progeny. How Socrates and Plato still Captivate the Modern Mind* (London, 2002), pp. 97–134.

7 Tessitore, Aristide (ed.), *Aristotle and Modern Politics. The Persistence of Political Philosophy* (Notre Dame, 2002); Goodman, Lenn E. and Talisse, Robert B. (eds.), *Aristotle's Politics Today* (Albany, 2007).

8 Schellhase, Kenneth C., *Tacitus in Renaissance Political Thought* (Chicago, 1976).

9 *The Adventures of Telemachus, Son of Ulysses* (Paris, 1699).

10 *Entretiens de Phocion* (Paris, 1763); see Wright, Johnson K., *A Classical Republican in Eighteenth-Century France. The Political Thought of Mably* (Stanford, 1997), pp. 80–93.

11 Shalev, Eran, 'Ancient masks, American Fathers: Classical pseudonyms during the American Revolution and Early Republic' *Journal of the Early Republic* 23:2 (2003), pp. 151–172.

12 Wrigley, Richard, 'Transformations of a revolutionary emblem: The liberty cap in the French Revolution' *French History* 11:2 (1997), pp. 131–169.

13 Rawson, Elizabeth, *The Spartan Tradition in European Thought* (Oxford, 1969).

14 Pocock, John G. A., *Barbarism and Religion. Volume III: The First Decline and Fall* (Cambridge, 2003).

15 Turner, Frank M. 'British politics and the demise of the Roman Republic: 1700–1939' *Historical Journal* 29 (1986), pp. 577–599.

NOTES

16 Matthie, William, 'Justice and the question of regimes in ancient and modern political philosophy: Aristotle and Hobbes' *Canadian Journal of Political Science* 9 (1976), pp. 449–463.

17 Rahe, Paul A., *Republics, Ancient and Modern* (Chapel Hill and London, 1994).

18 See for example Ober, Josiah and Manville, Brook, *Company of Citizens: What the World's First Democracy Teaches Leaders about Creating Great Organizations* (Cambridge, Mass., 2003).

19 Elster, Jon, 'Accountability in Athenian politics' in B. Manin, A. Przeworski and S. Stokes (eds.), *Democracy, Accountability and Representation* (Cambridge, 1998).

20 See Porter, James I. (ed.) *Classical Pasts: The Classical Traditions of Greece and Rome* (Princeton, NJ, 2006).

21 Nelson, Eric, *The Hebrew Republic: Jewish Sources and the Transformation of European Political Thought* (Cambridge, Mass., forthcoming). See Campos Boralevi, Lea, 'Classical foundation myths of European republicanism: the Jewish Commonwealth' in M. van Gelderen and Q. Skinner (eds.) *Republicanism. A Shared European Heritage. Vol. I* (Cambridge, 2002); Strumia, Anna, *L'imaginazione repubblicana. Sparta e Israele nel dibattito filosofico-politico dell' età di Cromwell* (Turin, 1991).

22 For a Roman focus, see Hammer, Dean, *Roman Political Thought and the Modern Theoretical Imagination* (Norman, 2008).

23 See Vlassopoulos, Kostas, 'The construction of antiquity and modernity in the eighteenth century: alterity, proximity, distantiation, immanency', in L. Foxhall and H.-J. Gehrke (eds) *Intentionale Geschichte – Spinning Time* (Stuttgart, 2009); Levine, Joseph M. *The Battle of the Books: History and Literature in the Augustan Age* (Ithaca, NY, 1991)

24 Hansen, Mogens H., *Polis: An Introduction to the Greek City-State* (Oxford, 2006); Vlassopoulos, Kostas, *Unthinking the Greek Polis. Ancient Greek History beyond Eurocentrism* (Cambridge, 2007), pp. 68–84.

25 Schofield, Malcolm, 'Euboulia in the Iliad', *Classical Quarterly* 36 (1986), pp. 6–31.

26 Lewis, John, *Solon the Thinker. Political Thought in Archaic Athens* (London, 2006), pp. 42–59.

27 Raaflaub, Kurt A., 'Poets, lawgivers and the beginnings of political reflection in archaic Greece' in C. Rowe and M. Schofield (eds.), *The Cambridge History of Greek and Roman Political Thought* (Cambridge, 2000).

Chapter I

1 Wiedemann, Thomas, 'Reflections of Roman political thought in Latin historical writing' in C. Rowe and M. Schofield (eds.), *The Cambridge History of Greek and Roman Political Thought* (Cambridge, 2000), pp. 517–519.

2 The most important texts can be found in Gagarin, Michael and Woodruff, Paul (eds.), *Early Greek Political Thought from Homer to the Sophists* (Cambridge, 1995).

3 Meier, Christian, *The Greek Discovery of Politics* (Cambridge, Mass. and London, 1990), pp. 157–185.

4 Meier, *Greek Discovery*, 29–52. Later on though *isonomia* would become essentially an equivalent to democracy.

5 Farrar, Cynthia, 'Ancient Greek political theory as a response to democracy' in J. Dunn (ed.), *Democracy: The Unfinished Journey, 508 BCE to CE 1993* (Oxford, 1992).

6 Old Oligarch, *Constitution of the Athenians*, 1.2. See Osborne, Robin (ed.), *The Old Oligarch: Pseudo-Xenophon's Constitution of the Athenians* (London, 2004).

7 Sinclair, Robert K., *Democracy and Participation in Athens* (Cambridge, 1988).

8 Rowe, Christopher, 'Aristotelian constitutions' in Rowe and Schofield, *The Cambridge History of Greek and Roman Political Thought*.

9 Aristotle, *Politics*, 1279b35 – 1280a3.

10 Plato, *Republic*, 562b-563e.

11 Herodotus, *Histories*, 3.80.

12 Hansen, Mogens H., *The Athenian Democracy in the Age of Demosthenes* (Oxford, 1991), pp. 225–246.

13 See Manin, Bernard, *The Principles of Representative Government* (Cambridge, 1997), pp. 8–41.

14 Hansen, Mogens H., 'The political powers of the People's Court in fourth-century Athens' in O. Murray and S. Price (eds), *The Greek City from Homer to Alexander* (Oxford, 1990).

15 Nippel, Wilfried, *Mischverfassungstheorie und Verfassungsrealität in Antike und früher Neuzeit* (Stuttgart, 1980).

16 See e.g. Aristotle, *Politics*, book vi.

17 Hodkinson, Stephen, 'The imaginary Spartan *politeia*' in M. H. Hansen (ed.), *The Imaginary Polis* (Copenhagen, 2005).

18 See Plato, *Laws*, 712d – 713a.

19 Andrews, Anthony, 'The government of classical Sparta' in M. Whitby (ed.), *Sparta* (New York, 2002).

20 Lintott, Andrew W., *The Constitution of the Roman Republic* (Oxford, 1999).

21 Nicolet, Claude, *The World of the Citizen in Republican Rome* (Berkeley and Los Angeles, 1980), pp. 207–315.

22 Millar, Fergus, *The Roman Republic in Political Thought* (Hanover and London, 2002).

23 Walbank, Frank W., *Polybius* (Berkeley and Los Angeles, 1972).

24 Polybius, *Histories*, VI.3–4.

25 Aristotle, *Politics*, 1265b35–41; 1294b13–34.

26 Aristotle, *Politics*, 1270b5 – 1271a7.

27 Nippel, Wilfried, 'Ancient and modern republicanism: "mixed constitution" and "ephors"' in B. Fontana (ed.), *The Invention of the Modern Republic* (Cambridge, 1994).

28 Herodotus, *Histories*, 3.82.

29 Ryffel, Heinrich, *Metabole politeion: Der Wandel der Staatsverfassungen* (Berne, 1949).

30 Plato, *Republic*, VIII.

31 Hahm, David E., 'Polybius's applied political theory' in A. Laks and

M. Schofield, (eds.), *Justice and Generosity. Studies in Hellenistic Social and Political Philosophy* (Cambridge, 1995).

32 Millar, *Roman Republic*, pp. 135–182.

33 Lintott, Andrew W., 'The theory of the mixed constitution at Rome' in J. Barnes and M. Griffin (eds.), *Philosophia Togata II* (Oxford, 1997).

34 See Millar, *Roman Republic*.

35 Schofield, Malcolm, 'Cicero's definition of *Res Publica*' in J. G. F. Powell (ed.) *Cicero the Philosopher* (Oxford, 1995).

36 Cicero, *Republic*, I.41–2

37 Tacitus, *Annals*, I.3.

38 O'Neill, James L., *The Origins and Development of Ancient Greek Democracy* (Lanham, MD, 1995), p. 104.

39 For the influence of classical political thought in the later Middle Ages, see Blythe, James M., '"Civic humanism" and medieval political thought' in J. Hankins (ed.), *Renaissance Civic Humanism: Reappraisals and Reflections* (Cambridge, 2000).

40 Molho, Anthony, Raaflaub, Kurt and Emlen, Julia (eds.), *City-States in Classical Antiquity and Medieval Italy* (Ann Arbor, 1991).

41 Grafton, Anthony, 'Humanism and political theory' in H. Burns and M. Goldie (eds.), *The Cambridge History of Political Thought 1450–1700* (Cambridge, 1991).

42 For the connection between the Roman image of monarchy and Machiavelli's *Prince*, see Stacey, Peter, *Roman Monarchy and the Renaissance Prince* (Cambridge, 2007), pp. 207–311.

43 Coby, Patrick, *Machiavelli's Romans: Liberty and Greatness in The Discourses on Livy* (Lanham MD, 1999).

44 Fink, Zera S., *The Classical Republicans. An Essay in the Recovery of a Pattern of Thought in Seventeenth-Century England* (Evanston, Ill., 1945).

45 Van Gelderen, Martin, 'Aristotelians, monarchomachs and republicans: Sovereignty and *respublica mixta* in Dutch and German political thought, 1580–1650' and Bödeker, Hans E., 'Debating the *respublica mixta*: German and Dutch political discourses around 1700' in M. van Gelderen and Q. Skinner (eds.) *Republicanism. A Shared European Heritage. Vol. I* (Cambridge, 2002).

46 Machiavelli, Niccolò, *The Discourses* (London, 1970), I.5, pp. 115–116.

47 The question of whether ancient Rome can be meaningfully characterised as a democracy has exercised modern scholars. See Millar, Fergus, *The Crowd in Rome in the Late Republic* (Ann Arbor, 1998); Mouritsen, Henrik, *Plebs and Politics in the Late Roman Republic* (Cambridge, 2001); Ward, Allen M., 'How democratic was the Roman Republic?' *New England Classical Journal* 31:2 (2004), pp. 101–119.

48 Machiavelli, *Discourses* , I.2, pp. 110–111.

49 McCormick, John P., 'Machiavellian democracy: Controlling elites with ferocious populism' *The American Political Science Review* 95 (2001), pp. 297–313.

50 McCuaig, William, *Carlo Sigonio. The Changing World of the Late Renaissance* (Princeton, NJ, 1989), pp. 224–250.

51 Roberts, Jennifer T., *Athens on Trial. The Antidemocratic Tradition in Western Thought* (Princeton, NJ, 1994).

52 Wootton, David, 'The true origins of republicanism or *de vera respublica*' in M. Albertone (ed.), *Il repubblicanesimo moderno: L'idea di repubblica nella riflessione storica di Franco Venturi* (Naples, 2006).

53 Levillain, Charles-Edouard, 'William III's military and political career in Neo-Roman context, 1672–1702' *The Historical Journal* 48 (2005), pp. 321–350.

54 Scott, Jonathan, *Commonwealth Principles. Republican Writings of the English Revolution* (Cambridge, 2004).

55 Worden, Blair, 'Marchamont Nedham and the beginnings of English republicanism 1649–1656' in D. Wootton (ed.), *Republicanism, Liberty, and Commercial Society, 1649–1776* (Stanford, 1994).

56 *The Excellencie of a Free State* (London, 1767), p. xvi.

57 Worden, Blair, 'Harrington's Oceana: Origins and aftermath' in Wootton, *Republicanism, Liberty, and Commercial Society.*

58 Harrington, *The Political Works of James Harrington* (Cambridge, 1977), pp. 163–164.

59 Neville, Henry, 'Plato Redidivus or a dialogue concerning government' and Moyle, Walter, 'An essay upon the constitution of the Roman government' in Robbins, Caroline (ed.), *Two English Republican Tracts* (Cambridge, 1969).

60 Robbins, *Two English Republican Tracts*, pp. 228–230, 237.

61 Robbins, *Two English Republican Tracts*, p. 91.

62 Shklar, Judith, 'Montesquieu and the new republicanism', in G. Bock (eds.), *Machiavelli and Republicanism* (Cambridge, 1990).

63 Cambiano, Giuseppe, 'Montesquieu e le antiche repubbliche greche' *Rivista di filosofia* 65 (1974), pp. 93–144.

64 Montesquieu, *Spirit of Laws*, XI.8, pp. 167–168.

65 Montesquieu, *Spirit of Laws*, V.3, p. 43.

66 Levy, Jacob T., 'Beyond Publius: Montesquieu, liberal republicanism and the small-republic thesis' *History of Political Thought* 27 (2006), pp. 50–90.

67 Translated as *Considerations on the Causes of the Greatness of the Romans and their Decline* (Indianapolis, 1999).

68 Rousseau, Jean-Jacques, *The Social Contract and Discourses* (London, 1973), III.4, p. 218.

69 Rousseau, *The Social Contract*, II.4, p. 187.

70 McCormick, John P., 'Rousseau's Rome and the repudiation of populist republicanism' *Critical Review of International Social and Political Philosophy* 10 (2007), pp. 3–27.

71 Rousseau, *The Social Contract*, III.15, pp. 240–241.

72 Rousseau, *The Social Contract*, III.12, p. 236.

73 Richard, Carl J., *The Founders and the Classics: Greece, Rome, and the American Enlightenment* (Cambridge, Mass., 1994); Nippel, Wilfried, *Antike oder Moderne Freiheit? Die Begründung der Demokratie in Athen und in der Neuzeit* (Frankfurt am Main, 2008), pp. 125–200.

74   Gueniffey, Patrice, 'Cordeliers and Girondins: the prehistory of the republic?' in B. Fontana, *Invention of the Republic*.

75   Hammersley, Rachel, *French Revolutionaries and English Republicans. The Cordeliers Club, 1790–1794* (Woodbridge and New York, 2005).

76   Wood, Gordon S., *The Creation of the American Republic 1776–1787* (Chapel Hill and London, 1969), p. 232.

77   Thompson, C. Bradley, 'John Adams's Machiavellian moment' *The Review of Politics* 57 (1995), pp. 389–417.

78   Quoted in Wood, *The Creation of the American Republic*, p. 230.

79   Hamilton, Alexander, Madison, James and Jay, John, *The Federalist with the Letters of 'Brutus'* (Cambridge, 2003), no. 10, pp. 43–44.

80   *The Federalist*, no. 10, p. 44.

81   *The Federalist*, no. 63, p. 309.

82   Less elitist supporters of representation, like Thomas Paine, were claiming just this: 'It is on this system that the American government is founded. It is representation ingrafted upon democracy. It has fixed the form by a scale parallel in all cases to the extent of the principle. What Athens was in miniature America will be in magnitude. The one was the wonder of the ancient world; the other is becoming the admiration of the present. . . It is preferable to simple democracy even in small territories. Athens, by representation, would have outrivalled her own democracy': 'The Rights of Man' in *Collected Writings* (New York, 1995), p. 568.

83   *The Federalist*, no. 10, p. 44.

84   Wood, Ellen M., 'Demos versus "We, the People": Freedom and democracy ancient and modern' in J. Ober and C. Hedrick (eds.), *Demokratia: A Conversation on Democracies, Ancient and Modern* (Princeton N.J., 1996).

85   Rosanvallon, Pierre, 'The history of the word "democracy" in France', *Journal of Democracy* 6:4 (1995), pp. 140–154.

86   See e.g. Velema, W. R. E., 'Republican readings of Montesquieu: *The Spirit of the Laws* in the Dutch Republic', *History of Political Thought* 18 (1997), pp. 43–63.

87   Wolin, Sheldon, *Tocqueville Between Two Worlds. The Making of a Political and Theoretical Life* (Princeton, NJ, 2001).

88   Richter, Melvin, 'The uses of theory: Tocqueville's adaptation of Montesquieu.' in M. Richter (ed.), *Essays in Theory and History: An Approach to the Social Sciences* (Cambridge, Mass., 1970).

89   Rosanvallon, Pierre, *Le sacre du citoyen. Histoire du suffrage universel en France* (Paris, 1992); pp. 331–350; idem, 'The republic of universal suffrage' in B. Fontana, *Invention of Republic*.

90   *Democracy Vindicated. An Essay on the Constitution and Government of the Roman State* (Norwich, 1796), p. iv.

91   Hampsher-Monk, Iain, 'John Thelwall and the eighteenth-century radical response to political economy', *The Historical Journal* 34 (1991), p. 2.

92   Turner, Frank, M., *The Greek Heritage in Victorian Britain* (New Haven and London, 1981), pp. 187–234.

93   Grote, George, *A History of Greece: From the Time of Solon to 403 BCE* (London and New York, 2001).

94 Manin, *Principles*, pp. 70–79.
95 Manin, *Principles*, pp. 79–93.
96 Hansen, Mogens H., *The Tradition of Ancient Greek Democracy and its Importance for Modern Democracy* (Copenhagen, 2005).
97 Bourke, Richard, 'Enlightenment, revolution and democracy' *Constellations* 15 (2008), pp. 10–32.

Chapter II

1   Constant, Benjamin, *Political Writings* (Cambridge, 1988), p. 311.
2   Constant, *Political Writings*, pp. 316–317.
3   Berlin, Isaiah, *Four Essays on Liberty* (Oxford, 1969).
4   See the doctoral thesis of Edge, Matthew E., *The Road to Modern Liberty: Freedom and Democracy Athenian and Modern* (Cambridge, 2006).
5   The idea that positive freedom is a separate species of freedom has been contested by Nelson, Eric, 'Liberty: One concept too many?' *Political Theory* 33 (2005), pp. 58–78. Nevertheless, the concept of freedom as self-mastery as a distinct view of freedom, compared e.g. with freedom as non-interference, is still valid.
6   Vlassopoulos, Kostas, 'Greek slavery: from domination to property and back again', forthcoming in the *Journal of Hellenic Studies* 130 (2010).
7   Lewis, John, *Solon the Thinker. Political Thought in Archaic Athens* (London, 2006), pp. 108–130.
8   Raaflaub, Kurt, *The Discovery of Freedom in Ancient Greece* (Chicago and London, 2004), pp. 58–89.
9   Raaflaub, Kurt A., 'Democracy, oligarchy, and the concept of the "free citizen" in late fifth-century Athens', *Political Theory* 11 (1983), pp. 517–544.
10 Demosthenes, *Against Timocrates*, 5.
11 Hypereides, Fragment D, 15.
12 Hansen, Mogens H., 'The ancient Athenian and the modern liberal view of liberty as a democratic ideal' in J. Ober and C. W. Hedrick, (eds), *Demokratia. A Conversation on Democracies, Ancient and Modern* (Princeton, NJ, 1996).
13 Thucydides, *History*, 2. 37.
14 Aristotle, *Politics*, 1317a41– b17.
15 Liddel, Peter, *Civic Obligation and Individual Liberty in Ancient Athens* (Oxford, 2007).
16 For a different view, see Miller, Fred D., *Nature, Justice and Rights in Aristotle's Politics* (Oxford, 1995).
17 Burnyeat, Miles F., 'Did the Ancient Greeks have the concept of human rights?', *Polis* 13 (1994), pp. 1–11.
18 Wallace, Robert W., 'Law, freedom and the concept of citizen's rights in democratic Athens' in Ober and Hedrick, *Demokratia*.
19 *Republic*, 563b-c.
20 Stalley, R. F., 'Plato's doctrine of freedom', *Proceedings of the Aristotelian Society* 98 (1998), pp. 45–58.
21 Wirszubski, Chaim, *Libertas as a Political Idea at Rome during the Late Republic and Early Principate* (Cambridge, 1950).

22 Livy, 1.2.1.

23 Raaflaub, Kurt, 'Freiheit in Athen und Rom: Ein Beispiel divergierender politischer Begriffsentwicklung in der Antike', *Historische Zeitschrift* 238 (1984), pp. 529–567.

24 Raaflaub, Kurt A. (ed.), *Social Struggles in Archaic Rome. New Perspectives on the Conflict of the Orders* (Malden and Oxford, 2005).

25 Livy, 3.45.8.

26 Herodotus, *Histories*, 5.78.

27 Raaflaub, *Discovery of Freedom*, pp. 181–193.

28 Herodotus, *Histories*, 9.122.

29 Sallust, *The Conspiracy of Catiline*, 7.

30 Tacitus, *Life of Agricola*, 3.

31 Skinner, Quentin, *The Foundations of Modern Political Thought. Volume I: The Renaissance* (Cambridge, 1978), pp. 3–65.

32 Baron, Hans, *The Crisis of the Early Italian Renaissance. Civic Humanism and Republican Liberty in an Age of Classicism and Tyranny* (Princeton, NJ, 1955).

33 Hörnqvist, Michael, *Machiavelli and Empire* (Cambridge, 2004).

34 Machiavelli, Niccolò, *The Discourses* (London, 1970), I.6, pp. 118–124.

35 Armitage, David, 'Empire and liberty: a republican dilemma' in M. van Gelderen and Q. Skinner (eds.) *Republicanism. A Shared European Heritage. Vol. II* (Cambridge, 2002).

36 *Discourses*, II.2, p. 275.

37 Skinner, Quentin, *The Foundations of Modern Political Thought. Volume II: The Age of Reformation* (Cambridge, 1978).

38 Nippel, Wilfried, 'Ancient and modern republicanism: "mixed constitution" and "ephors"' in B. Fontana (ed.), *The Invention of the Modern Republic* (Cambridge, 1994).

39 Catalano, Pierangelo, *Tribunato e resistenza* (Turin, 1971).

40 Skinner, Quentin, 'Classical liberty and the coming of the English Civil War' in Skinner and van Gelderen, *Republicanism, Volume II*.

41 Hobbes, Thomas, *Leviathan* (Cambridge, 1991), pp. 149–150.

42 Skinner, Quentin, *Hobbes and Republican Liberty* (Cambridge, 2008).

43 Hobbes, *Leviathan*, p. 149.

44 On Roman law and political thought, see Johnston, David, 'The jurists' in C. Rowe and M. Schofield (eds.) *The Cambridge History of Greek and Roman Political Thought* (Cambridge, 2000).

45 *Digest*, 1.1.10.

46 Gobetti, Daniela, *Private and Public. Individuals, Households and Body Politic in Locke and Hutcheson* (London, 1992). See also Gilmore, M. P., *Arguments from Roman Law in Political Thought, 1200–1600* (Cambridge, MA, 1941).

47 Stein, Peter, *Roman Law in European History* (Cambridge, 1999).

48 Tuck, Richard, *Natural Rights Theories: Their Origin and Development* (Cambridge, 1979); Garnsey, Peter, *Thinking About Property. From Antiquity to the Age of Revolution* (Cambridge, 2007), pp. 208–232.

49 See also Straumann, Benjamin, '"Ancient Caesarian lawyers" in a state of nature: Natural tradition and human rights in Hugo Grotius *De iurae praedae*', *Political Theory* 34 (2006), pp. 328–350.

50 Skinner, Quentin, *Liberty before Liberalism* (Cambridge, 1998).
51 Nedham, Marchamont, *The Excellencie of a Free State* (London, 1767), pp. 39–44.
52 Nedham, *Excellencie*, p. 11.
53 Zuckert, Michael P., *Natural Rights and the New Republicanism* (Princeton, NJ, 1994), pp. 170–183.
54 Weinbrot, Howard D., *Augustus Caesar in 'Augustan' England. The Decline of a Classical Norm* (Princeton, NJ, 1978).
55 *The Works of Tacitus* (London, 1737).
56 *Cato's Letters* (Indianapolis, 1995).
57 Gunn, John A. W., *Beyond Liberty and Property. The Process of Self-Recognition in Eighteenth-Century Political Thought* (Kingston, 1983), pp. 7–42.
58 Ward, Lee, *The Politics of Liberty in England and Revolutionary America* (Cambridge, 2004).
59 Adams, John, *The Works of John Adams. Vol. IV* (Boston, 1856), p. 15.
60 Sellers, M. N. S., *American Republicanism: Roman Ideology in the United States Constitution* (New York, 1994).
61 Myers, Roger, 'Montesquieu on the causes of Roman greatness' *History of Political Thought* 16 (1995), pp. 37–47; Rahe, Paul A., 'The book that never was: Montesquieu's *Considerations on the Romans* in historical context' *History of Political Thought* 26 (2005), pp. 43–89.
62 Montesquieu, *The Spirit of the Laws* (Cambridge, 1989), XI.3–4, pp. 155–156.
63 Sullivan, Vickie B., 'Against the despotism of a republic: Montesquieu's correction of Machiavelli in the name of the security of the individual', *History of Political Thought* 27 (2006), pp. 263–289.
64 Avlami, Chrysanthi, 'Libertà liberale contro libertà antica. Francia e Inghilterra, 1752–1856' in S. Settis (ed.), *I Greci. Storia, Cultura, Arte, Società III* (Turin, 2002).
65 Guerci, Luciano, *Libertà degli antichi e libertà dei moderni. Sparta, Atene e i 'philosophes' nella Francia del' 700* (Naples, 1979).
66 Cambiano, Giuseppe, *Polis. Un modello per la cultura europea* (Rome and Bari, 2007), pp. 312–369.
67 Ferguson, Adam, *An Essay on the History of Civil Society* (Cambridge, 1995), pp. 176–177.
68 Robertson, John, 'The Scottish Enlightenment at the limits of the civic tradition' in I. Hont and M. Ignatieff (eds.) *Wealth and Virtue. The Shaping of Political Economy in the Scottish Enlightenment* (Cambridge, 1983).
69 Hume, David, 'Of the populousness of ancient nations' in *Selected Essays* (Oxford, 1993), pp. 226–277.
70 Rousseau, Jean-Jacques, *The Social Contract and Discourses* (London, 1973), I.1, p. 165.
71 Rousseau, Jean Jacques, *Letter to Beaumont, Letters Written from the Mountain, and Related Writings* (Hanover, NH, 2001), p. 292.
72 Wokler, Robert, 'Rousseau's two concepts of liberty' in G. Feaver and F. Rosen (eds.), *Lives, Liberties and the Public Good. New Essays in Political Theory for Maurice Cranston* (Basingstoke and London, 1987).

73 Spitz, Jean-Fabien, *La liberté politique: essai de généalogie conceptuelle* (Paris, 1995).

74 Rousseau, Jean Jacques, 'Discourse on the Arts and Sciences' in *The Social Contract and Discourses* (London, 1973).

75 Hammersley, Rachel, *French Revolutionaries and English Republicans. The Cordeliers Club, 1790–1794* (Woodbridge and New York, 2005).

76 Saige, Guillaume-Joseph, *Caton, ou Entretien sur la liberté et les vertus politiques* (London, 1770).

77 Baker, Keith M., *Inventing the French Revolution. Essays in French Political Culture in the Eighteenth Century* (Cambridge, 1990), pp. 31–85, 128–152.

78 Baker, Keith M. 'Transformations of classical republicanism in eighteenth-century France', *Journal of Modern History* 73 (2001), pp. 32–53.

79 Hartog, Francois, 'La Révolution française et l'Antiquité. Avenir d'une illusion ou cheminement d'un quiproquo?' in C. Avlami (ed.), *L'antiquité grecque au XIXe siècle: un exemplum contesté?* (Paris 2000).

80 Kalyvas, Andreas and Katznelson, Ira, *Liberal Beginnings: Making a Republic for the Moderns* (Cambridge, 2008), pp. 146–175.

81 Hulliung, Mark, *Citizens and Citoyens: Republicans and Liberals in America and France* (Cambridge, Mass., 2002), pp. 9–16.

82 Geuss, Raymond, *History and Illusion in Politics* (Cambridge, 2001), 131–152.

83 Williams, Bernard, *Shame and Necessity* (Berkeley and Oxford, 1993), p. 125.

84 Terray, Emmanuel, 'Equality in Hellenic and modern days' in R.-P. Droit (ed.), *Greeks and Romans in the Modern World* (Boulder, 1998).

85 Pettit, Philip, *Republicanism. A Theory of Freedom and Government* (Oxford, 1999).

86 Mill, John S., 'Grote's History of Greece, II' in *Collected Works of John Stuart Mill, Vol. 11: Essays on Philosophy and the Classics* (Toronto and London, 1978), p. 319.

87 Liddel, Peter, 'Liberty and obligations in George Grote's Athens', *Polis* 23 (2006), pp. 140–161.

88 Kymlicka, Will, *Contemporary Political Philosophy. An Introduction* (Oxford, 2002), pp. 377–398.

89 Steinberger, Peter J., 'Public and private', *Political Studies* 47 (1999), pp. 292–313.

Chapter III

1 Hodkinson, Stephen, 'The development of Spartan society and institutions in the archaic period' in L. G. Mitchell and P. J. Rhodes (eds.), *The Development of the Polis in Archaic Greece* (London, 1997).

2 On the political ideology expressed in the Athenian funeral orations, see Loraux, Nicole, *The Invention of Athens. The Funeral Oration in the Classical City* (Cambridge, Mass., 1986).

3 Thucydides, *History*, 2.40.

4 Liddel, Peter, *Civic Obligation and Individual Liberty in Ancient Athens* (Oxford, 2007).

5   Adkins, Arthur W. H., *Merit and Responsibility. A Study in Greek Values* (Oxford, 1960), pp. 195–219.

6   Whitehead, David, 'Cardinal Virtues: the language of public approbation in democratic Athens', *Classica et Mediaevalia* 44 (1993), pp. 37–75.

7   Thucydides, *History*, 2.37.

8   Hansen, Mogens H., *The Athenian Democracy in the Age of Demosthenes* (Oxford, 1991), pp. 125–160.

9   Connor, William R., *The New Politicians of Fifth-Century Athens* (Princeton, N.J., 1971).

10   Herodotus, *Histories*, 5.97.

11   Loraux, Nicole, *The Divided City. On Memory and Forgetting in Ancient Athens* (New York, 2002); eadem, *La tragédie d'Athènes: la politique entre l'ombre et l'utopie* (Paris, 2005).

12   Finley, Moses I., *Democracy Ancient and Modern* (London, 1985), pp. 45–46.

13   Finkelberg, Margalit, 'Virtue and circumstances: On the city-state concept of arete', *American Journal of Philology* 123 (2002), pp. 35–49.

14   Ostwald, Martin, *From Popular Sovereignty to the Sovereignty of Law. Law, Society, and Politics in Fifth-Century Athens* (Berkeley and London, 1986).

15   Hansen, *The Athenian Democracy in the Age of Demosthenes*, pp. 205–212.

16   Ober, Josiah, 'The debate over civic education in classical Athens' in Y. Lee Too (ed.) *Education in Greek and Roman Antiquity* (Leiden, 2001).

17   Ober, Josiah, *Political Dissent in Democratic Athens. Intellectual Critics of Popular Rule* (Princeton, NJ, 1998).

18   Ober, Josiah, 'Thucydides and the invention of political science' in A. Rengakos and A. Tsakmakis (eds.) *Brill's Companion to Thucydides* (Leiden and Boston, 2006).

19   Price, Jonathan J., *Thucydides and Internal War* (Cambridge, 2001).

20   Thucydides, *History*, 3.82.

21   Yunis, Harvey, *Taming Democracy. Models of Political Rhetoric in Classical Athens* (Ithaca and London, 1996), pp. 59–116.

22   Plato, *Protagoras*, 319b-d.

23   Schofield, Malcolm, *Plato: Political Philosophy* (Oxford, 2006), pp. 136–193.

24   Kraut, Richard, *Aristotle: Political Philosophy* (Oxford, 2002).

25   *Politics*, 1253a8–18.

26   *Politics*, 1275b18–20.

27   *Politics*, 1259a37– 1260a20.

28   Newell, W. R., 'Superlative virtue: The problem of monarchy in Aristotle's *Politics*', *Western Political Quarterly* 40 (1987), pp. 159–178.

29   Mulgan, Richard, 'Aristotle and the value of political participation', *Political Theory* 18 (1990), pp. 195–215.

30   Yack, Bernard, *The Problems of a Political Animal. Community, Justice and Conflict in Aristotelian Political Thought* (Berkeley, Los Angeles and London, 1993).

31   Adamovsky, Ezequiel, 'Aristotle, Diderot, liberalism and the idea of the "middle class": A comparison of two contexts of emergence of a metaphorical formation', *History of Political Thought* 26 (2005), pp. 303–333.

32   Biondi, Carrie-Ann, 'Aristotle on the mixed constitution and its relevance for

American political thought', *Social Philosophy and Policy* 24 (2007), pp. 176–198.

33 *Politics*, 1291b31 – 1292a37.

34 Nippel, Wilfried, 'Ancient and modern republicanism: "mixed constitution" and "ephors"' in B. Fontana (ed.), *The Invention of the Modern Republic* (Cambridge, 1994), p. 9.

35 Earl, Donald, *The Moral and Political Tradition of Rome* (London, 1967).

36 See Tuck, Richard, *Philosophy and Government 1572–1651* (Cambridge, 1993), pp. 6–12.

37 Long, Anthony A., 'Cicero's politics in *De officiis*' in A. Laks and M. Schofield, (eds), *Justice and Generosity. Studies in Hellenistic Social and Political Philosophy* (Cambridge, 1995).

38 Fantham, Elaine, *The Roman World of Cicero's De Oratore* (Oxford, 2004).

39 Cicero, *Republic*, I.1–2.

40 Moore, T. J. *Artistry and Ideology. Livy's Vocabulary of Virtue* (Frankfurt, 1989).

41 Aalders, G. J. D. *Plutarch's Political Thought* (Amsterdam, Oxford and New York, 1982); Duff, Timothy E., *Plutarch's Lives: Exploring Virtue and Vice* (Oxford, 2002).

42 Griffin, Miriam, 'Seneca and Pliny' in C. Rowe and M. Schofield (eds.), *The Cambridge History of Greek and Roman Political Thought* (Cambridge, 2000).

43 Mellor, Ronald, *Tacitus* (New York and London, 1993), pp. 87–112.

44 Percival, John, 'Tacitus and the principate', *Greece & Rome* 27 (1980), pp. 119–133.

45 Stacey, Peter, *Roman Monarchy and the Renaissance Prince* (Cambridge, 2007).

46 Hankins, James (ed.), *Renaissance Civic Humanism: Reappraisals and Reflections* (Cambridge, 2000).

47 Baron, Hans, 'The memory of Cicero's Roman civic spirit in the medieval centuries and in the Florentine Renaissance' in *In Search of Florentine Civic Humanism. Essays on the Transition form Medieval to Modern Thought*, I (Princeton, NJ, 1988).

48 See e.g. Peltonen, Markku, *Classical Humanism and Republicanism in English Political Thought 1570–1640* (Cambridge, 1995).

49 Rahe, Paul A., 'Situating Machiavelli' in Hankins, *Renaissance Civic Humanism*.

50 Skinner, Quentin, *Machiavelli: A Very Short Introduction* (Oxford, 2000), p. 60.

51 On his recourse to an alternative ancient tradition, see Rahe, Paul A., 'In the shadow of Lucretius. The Epicurean foundations of Machiavelli's political thought', *History of Political Thought* 28 (2007), pp. 30–55.

52 Machiavelli, Niccolò, *The Discourses* (London, 1970), I.3, pp. 111–112.

53 *Discourses*, III.1, pp. 385–7.

54 Sullivan, Vickie B., *Machiavelli, Hobbes and the Formation of a Liberal Republicanism in England* (Cambridge, 2004), pp. 31–79.

55 On the connection between the *Prince* and ancient political thought, see Stacey, *Roman Monarchy*, pp. 207–311.

56 Miller, Peter N., *Defining the Common Good. Empire, Religion and Philosophy in Eighteenth-Century Britain* (Cambridge, 1994), pp. 21–87.

57 Burke, Peter, 'Tacitism, scepticism and reason of state' in J. H. Burns (ed.),

The Cambridge History of Political Thought 1450–1700 (Cambridge, 1991).

58   Schlatter, Richard (ed.), *Hobbes's Thucydides* (New Brunswick, 1975).

59   Slomp, Gabriella, 'Hobbes, Thucydides and The Three Greatest Things', *History of Political Thought* 11 (1990), pp. 565–586; Brown, Clifford Jr, 'Thucydides, Hobbes, and the derivation of anarchy', *History of Political Thought* 8 (1987), pp. 33–62.

60   Diesner, Hans-Joachim, 'Thukydides und Thomas Hobbes: Zur Strukturanalyse der Macht', *Historia* 29 (1980), pp. 1–16

61   Scott, Jonathan, 'The peace of silence. Thucydides and the English Civil War' in G. A. J. Roberts and T. Sorell (eds.), *Hobbes and History* (London and New York, 2000).

62   *Hobbes Thucydides*, p. 12.

63   Tuck, Richard, 'Hobbes and democracy' in A. Brett, J. Tully and H. Hamilton-Bleakley (eds.), *Rethinking the Foundations of Modern Political Thought* (Cambridge, 2006).

64   Rahe, Paul A., *Republics Ancient and Modern. Classical Republicanism and the American Revolution* (Chapel Hill, 1992), pp. 409–429; Scott, Jonathan, 'The Rapture of Motion: James Harrington's Republicanism' in N. Phillipson and Q. Skinner (eds.), *Political Discourse in Early Modern Europe* (Cambridge, 1993).

65   Harrington, James, *The Political Works of James Harrington* (Cambridge, 1977), p. 272.

66   Harrington, *Political Works*, p. 161.

67   Harrington, *Political Works*, p. 275.

68   Harrington, *Political Works*, p. 279; Remer, Gary, 'James Harrington's new deliberative rhetoric: Reflections of an anticlassical republicanism' *History of Political Thought* 16 (1995), pp. 532–557.

69   Harrington, *Political Works*, pp. 172–174.

70   Harrington, *Political Works*, p. 172.

71   Harrington, *Political Works*, p. 177.

72   Shklar, Judith, 'Montesquieu and the new republicanism' in G. Bock, Q. Skinner and M. Viroli (eds.), *Machiavelli and Republicanism* (Cambridge, 1990).

73   Montesquieu, *The Spirit of the Laws* (Cambridge, 1989), III.3, pp. 22–23.

74   *Spirit of Laws*, IV.4, p. 35.

75   Kalyvas, Andreas and Katznelson, Ira, *Liberal Beginnings: Making a Republic for the Moderns* (Cambridge, 2008), pp. 51–87.

76   Ferguson, Adam, *An Essay on the History of Civil Society* (Cambridge, 1995), p. 150.

77   Ferguson, Adam, *The History of the Progress and Termination of the Roman Republic. Vol. I* (London, 1783), p. 23.

78   Hamilton, Alexander, Madison, James and Jay, John, *The Federalist with the Letters of 'Brutus'* (Cambridge, 2003), no. 9, p. 35.

79   *The Federalist*, no. 55, p. 270.

80   *The Federalist*, no. 10, p. 127.

81   Kalyvas and Katznelson, *Liberal Beginnings*, pp. 88–117.

82   Rousseau, Jean Jacques, 'Considerations on the Government of Poland' in *Political Writings* (Madison, WI, 1986), p. 165.

83 Rousseau, Jean-Jacques, *The Social Contract and Discourses*, (London, 1973), IV.3, p. 185.

84 Rousseau, 'Discourse on Political Economy' in *The Social Contract*, p. 122.

85 Parker, Harold T., *The Cult of Antiquity and the French Revolutionaries. A Study in the Development of the Revolutionary Spirit* (Chicago, 1937), pp. 119–138.

86 Parker, *Cult of Antiquity*, pp. 146–147.

87 'Discours sur les principes de morale politique qui doivent guider la Convention nationale dans l'administration intérieure de la République', quoted in Baker, Keith M. 'Transformations of classical republicanism in eighteenth-century France', *Journal of Modern History* 73 (2001), p. 49.

88 Parker, *Cult of Antiquity*, pp. 133–136.

89 Quoted in Hammersley, Rachel, *French Revolutionaries and English Republicans. The Cordeliers Club, 1790–1794* (Woodbridge and New York, 2005), p. 152.

90 Macpherson, Crawford B., *The Life and Times of Liberal Democracy* (Oxford, 1977).

91 Urbinati, Nadia, *Mill on Democracy. From the Athenian Polis to Representative Government* (Chicago, 2002).

92 Mill, John S., 'Considerations on representative government' in *Collected Works of John Stuart Mill, Vol. 19: Essays on Politics and Society, Part II* (Toronto and London, 1977), p. 411.

93 Mill, John S., 'Grote's History of Greece, II' in *Collected Works of John Stuart Mill, Vol. 11: Essays on Philosophy and the Classics* (Toronto and London, 1978), pp. 323–324.

94 Biagini, Eugenio F., 'Liberalism and direct democracy: John Stuart Mill and the model of ancient Athens' in idem, (ed.), *Citizenship and Community. Liberals, Radicals and Collective Identities in the British Isles 1865–1931* (Cambridge, 1996), p. 38.

95 Mill, 'Considerations', p. 458.

96 Popper, Karl, *The Open Society and its Enemies. Vol. I: The Spell of Plato* (London, 1945).

97 The classic exposition of this view is Schumpeter, Joseph, *Capitalism, Socialism and Democracy* (London, 1943).

98 See Elster, Jon, 'The market and the forum. Three varieties of political theory' in J. Bohman and W. Rehg (eds), *Deliberative Democracy. Essays on Reason and Politics* (Cambridge, Mass. and London, 1997).

99 Arendt, Hannah, *The Human Condition* (Chicago, 1958).

100 Euben, J. Peter, 'Arendt's Hellenism' and Taminiaux, Jacques, 'Athens and Rome' in D. Villa (ed.), *The Cambridge Companion to Hannah Arendt* (Cambridge, 2001).

101 Labelle, Giles, 'Two refoundation projects of democracy in contemporary French philosophy. Cornelius Castoriadis and Jacques Rancière', *Philosophy and Social Criticism* 27:4 (2001), pp. 75–103.

102 But see e.g. Frank, Jill, *A Democracy of Distinction: Aristotle and the Work of Politics* (Chicago, 2005).

103 Collins, Susan D., *Aristotle and the Rediscovery of Citizenship* (Cambridge, 2006).

104 Yack, *The Problems of a Political Animal*; Garsten, Bryan, *Saving Persuasion. A Defence of Rhetoric and Judgement* (Cambridge, Mass., 2006).
105 Finley, *Democracy Ancient and Modern*.
106 Ober, Josiah, *Mass and Elite in Democratic Athens. Rhetoric, Ideology and the Power of the People* (Princeton, N. J., 1989).
107 Ober, Josiah, *Democracy and Knowledge. Innovation and Learning in Classical Athens* (Princeton and Oxford, 2008).
108 Mara, Gerald M., 'After virtue, autonomy: Jürgen Habermas and Greek political theory', *The Journal of Politics* 47 (1985), pp. 1036–1061.
109 Shiffman, Gary, 'Deliberation versus decision. Platonism in contemporary democratic theory' in B. Fontana, C. J. Nederman and G. Remer (eds), *Talking Democracy. Historical Perspectives on Rhetoric and Democracy* (University Park, 2004); Remer, Gary, 'Political oratory and conversation: Cicero versus deliberative democracy', *Political Theory* 27 (1999), pp. 39–64.
110 But see the interesting point of David Hume in 'Of some remarkable customs' in *Selected Essays* (Oxford, 1993), p. 218.

Chapter IV

1   Adkins, Arthur W. H., *Merit and Responsibility. A Study in Greek Values* (Oxford, 1960).
2   *Politics*, 1252b28–32.
3   *Politics*, 1280b1–9.
4   *Politics*, 1278b20–23.
5   Hodkinson, Stephen, 'The imaginary Spartan *politeia*' in M. H. Hansen (ed.), *The Imaginary Polis* (Copenhagen, 2005).
6   Xenophon, *Constitution of the Lacedaemonians*, 10.
7   Powell, Anton, *Athens and Sparta. Constructing Greek Political and Social History from 478 BCE* (New York, 2001) pp. 218–270.
8   Cartledge, Paul, 'Comparatively equal' in J. Ober and C. Hedrick (eds.), *Demokratia: A Conversation on Democracies, Ancient and Modern* (Princeton N.J., 1996).
9   Tigerstedt, Eugene N., *The Legend of Sparta in Classical Antiquity* (Stockholm, 1965–74); Rawson, Elizabeth, *The Spartan Tradition in European Thought* (Oxford, 1969).
10 Plato, *Laws*, 650b.
11 Klosko, George, *The Development of Plato's Political Theory* (London, 1986).
12 Tigerstedt, *The Legend of Sparta*, pp. 244–276.
13 Garnsey, Peter, *Thinking About Property. From Antiquity to the Age of Revolution* (Cambridge, 2007), pp. 6–30.
14 Tigerstedt, *The Legend of Sparta Vol II*.
15 Hodkinson, Stephen, 'Inheritance, marriage and demography: perspectives upon the success and decline of classical Sparta', in A. Powell (ed.), *Classical Sparta: Techniques behind her Success* (London, 1989).
16 An influential combination of the two views is Plutarch, *Life of Agis*, 5.
17 Cartledge, Paul and Spawforth, Anthony, *Hellenistic and Roman Sparta: A Tale of Two Cities* (London, 2002), pp. 35–53.

18 Hodkinson, Stephen, *Property and Wealth in Classical Sparta* (London, 2000), pp. 19–60.
19 Stockton, David, *The Gracchi* (Oxford, 1979).
20 Plutarch, *Life of Lycurgus*, 8.
21 *Life of Tiberius Gracchus*, 9.
22 Cicero, *On Duties*, II.78.
23 Cicero, *On Duties*, II.73.
24 Wood, Neal, *Cicero's Social and Political Thought* (Berkeley. Los Angeles and Oxford, 1988), pp. 128–132.
25 Nelson, Eric, *The Greek Tradition in Republican Thought* (Cambridge, 2004).
26 Feinberg, B. S., 'Creativity and the political community: The role of the lawgiver in the thought of Plato, Machiavelli and Rousseau', *Western Political Quarterly* 23 (1970), pp. 471–484.
27 Nelson, *Greek Tradition*, pp. 19–48.
28 More, Thomas, *Utopia* (Cambridge, 2005), pp. 35–36.
29 Manuel, Frank, E. and Manuel, Fritzie P., *Utopian Thought in the Western World* (Oxford, 1979).
30 Shklar, Judith, 'The political theory of utopia: From melancholy to nostalgia', *Daedalus* 94 (1965), pp. 367–381.
31 This explains why some modern scholars, led by philosopher Leo Strauss, have argued that the Utopia of the *Republic* was also only a moral standard and not a plan actually to be realized. See Strauss, Leo, *The City of Man* (Chicago, 1958), pp. 50–138.
32 Nelson, *Greek Tradition*, pp. 87–126.
33 Translated as *Telemachus* (Cambridge, 1994).
34 Riley, Patrick, 'Rousseau, Fénelon and the quarrel between the ancients and the moderns' in idem, (ed.), *The Cambridge Companion to Rousseau* (Cambridge, 2001).
35 Hont, Istvan. 'The early Enlightenment debate on commerce and luxury' in M. Goldie and R. Wokler, (eds.), *The Cambridge History of Eighteenth-Century Political Thought* (Cambridge, 2006).
36 Tuck, Richard, *Philosophy and Government 1572–1651* (Cambridge, 1993).
37 Pocock, John G. A., *The Machiavellian Moment. Florentine Political Thought and the Atlantic Republican Tradition* (Princeton, NJ, 1975), pp. 423–505.
38 Rosanvallon, Pierre, *Le capitalisme utopique. Critique de l'idéologie économique* (Paris, 1979).
39 Smith, Adam, *The Wealth of Nations*, (London, 1979), I.2, p. 119.
40 Paine, Thomas, 'Common Sense' in *Collected Writings* (New York, 1995), p. 6.
41 Ferguson, Adam, *An Essay on the History of Civil Society* (Cambridge, 1995), p. 121.
42 Rousseau, Jean-Jacques, 'Discourse on Political Economy' in *The Social Contract and Discourses* (London, 1973), p. 127.
43 Klosko, George, *Jacobins and Utopians. The Political Theory of Fundamental Moral Reform* (Notre Dame, 2003).
44 Shklar, Judith, 'Rousseau's two models: Sparta and the Age of Gold', *Political Science Quarterly* 81 (1966), pp. 25–51.

45 Rousseau, J. J., *Oeuvres complètes de Jean-Jacques Rousseau. Vol. III* (Paris, 1964), p. 83.

46 Yack, Bernard, *Longing for Total Revolution. Philosophical Sources of Social Discontent from Rousseau to Marx and Nietzsche* (Princeton, NJ, 1986), pp. 35–85.

47 Wright, Johnson K., *A Classical Republican in Eighteenth-Century France. The Political Thought of Mably* (Stanford, 1997).

48 Mably, Abbé de, *Observations on the Greeks* (Lynn, 1776), p. 24.

49 Hodkinson, Stephen, 'Five words that shook the world: Plutarch, Lykourgos 16 and appropriations of Spartan communal property ownership in eighteenth-century France' in N. Birgalias, K. Burazelis and P. Cartledge (eds.), *The Contribution of Ancient Sparta to Political Thought and Practice* (Athens, 2007).

50 Sonenscher, Michael, 'Property, community and citizenship' in Goldie and Wokler, *The Cambridge History of Eighteenth-Century Political Thought*.

51 Clauss, Manfred, 'Die Rezeption der Antike bei François-Noël (Camille-Gracchus) Babeuf', *Gymnasium* 86 (1979), pp. 81–94; Keaveney, Arthur, 'The three Gracchi: Tiberius, Caius and Babeuf' in *La storia della storiografia europea sulla rivoluzione francese* (Rome, 1990).

52 Rose, R. B. 'The "Red Scare" of the 1790s: The French Revolution and the "Agrarian Law"', *Past and Present* 103 (1984), pp. 113–130.

53 Momigliano, Arnaldo, 'New paths of classicism in the nineteenth century' in *Studies on Modern Scholarship* (Berkeley and Los Angeles, 1994), pp. 225–236.

54 Fleischacker, Samuel, *A Short History of Distributive Justice* (Cambridge, Mass, 2005), pp. 75–79.

55 Leopold, David, *The Young Karl Marx. German Philosophy, Modern Politics and Human Flourishing* (Cambridge, 2007), pp. 193–297; McCarthy, George E. (ed.), *Marx and Aristotle. Nineteenth-Century German Social Theory and Classical Antiquity* (Savage, MA, 1992).

56 Wisner, David A., *The Cult of the Legislator in France, 1750–1830. A Study in the Political Theology of the French Enlightenment* (Oxford, 1997).

57 Quoted in Geuss, Raymond, *Outside Ethics* (Princeton, NJ, 2005), p. 97.

58 Wokler, Robert, 'Ideology and the origins of social science' in Goldie and Wokler, *The Cambridge History of Eighteenth-Century Political Thought*.

59 Harris, Jose, 'Platonism, positivism and progressivism: aspects of British sociological thought in the early twentieth century' in E. F. Biagini, (ed.), *Citizenship and Community. Liberals, Radicals and Collective Identities in the British Isles 1865–1931* (Cambridge, 1996); Den Otter, Sandra M., *British Idealism and Social Explanation: A Study in Late Victorian Thought* (Oxford, 1996).

60 *A Theory of Justice* (Cambridge, Mass., 1971).

61 Kymlicka, Will, *Contemporary Political Philosophy. An Introduction* (Oxford, 2002).

62 Wallach, John R., 'Contemporary Aristotelianism', *Political Theory* 20 (1992), pp. 613–641.

63 Nussbaum, Martha, 'Aristotelian social democracy' in A. Tessitore (ed.), *Aristotle and Modern Politics. The Persistence of Political Philosophy* (Notre Dame, 2002).

64 Nelson, Eric, 'From primary goods to capabilities. Distributive justice and the problem of neutrality', *Political Theory* 36 (2008), p. 115.

Epilogue

1   Scott, Jonathan, *Commonwealth Principles. Republican Writings of the English Revolution* (Cambridge, 2004).
2   Brooke, Christopher, 'Rousseau's political philosophy: Stoic and Augustinian origins' in P. Riley (ed.), *The Cambridge Companion to Rousseau* (Cambridge, 2001).

Index